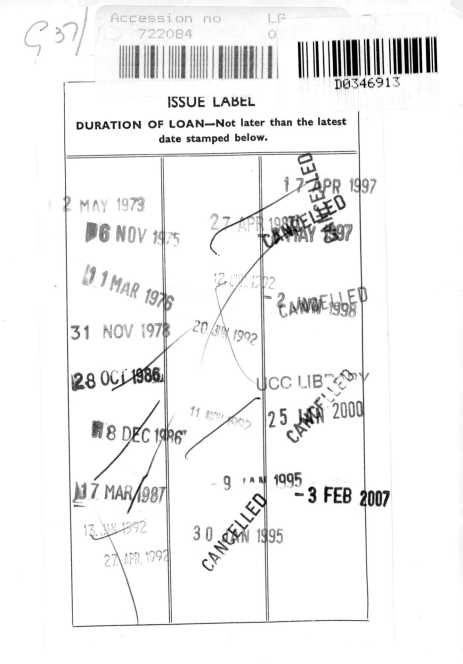

Methods of
Sociological Enquiry

BLACKWELL'S SOCIOLOGY SERIES
General Editor: Bryan R. Wilson

Published

POLITICS IN EVERYDAY LIFE
H. Victor Wiseman

THE SOCIOLOGICAL INTERPRETATION OF RELIGION
Roland Robertson

Forthcoming

SOCIETY, CULTURE AND PERSONALITY
Z. Barbu

Methods of Sociological Enquiry

PETER H. MANN

OXFORD

BASIL BLACKWELL

1971

© BASIL BLACKWELL, 1968

ISBN 0 631 09730 9 Cloth bound edition
ISBN 0 631 09720 1 Paper bound edition

Reprinted 1971

Printed in Great Britain by
COMPTON PRINTING LTD, LONDON AND AYLESBURY
AND BOUND BY
THE KEMP HALL BINDERY, OXFORD

Contents

Preface

Sociology today is both enjoying, and suffering from, a tremendous wave of interest both inside and outside the universities. Within the universities it has become one of the most popular subjects with undergraduates and outside the universities the general public has become accustomed to hearing and reading about sociological problems and sociological investigations. All this is very flattering to the sociologist who finds himself being asked to advise committees of this and that on how to conduct surveys and studies, and it is very pleasing for the university teacher to see his students going out into the world to undertake serious research studies. But this popularity carries with it the dangers of both amateurism and slap-dash workmanship. Amateurism is dangerous because 'social surveys' have become almost parlour games in some schools and voluntary organisations. Hastily contrived and badly executed surveys waste everyone's time and, when people associate them with serious sociology, they bring the discipline into disrepute. Slap-dash workmanship by people who do call themselves sociologists is even worse. The graduate sociologist who has never been taught some of the basic methods of enquiry barely deserves his title.

This book is very much an elementary introduction to methods of sociological enquiry, and it is intended for the beginner. By the time he has graduated, a university student ought to have gone on much further than this book attempts to go, and if the graduate can look back on this book and think how very simple it was then I shall feel I have succeeded in my task.

Sociology itself is a difficult subject since its field of enquiry is so broad. Yet it is fascinating because we live in societies and our data are all around us all the time. In my years as a sociologist I have met many different sorts of sociologists with a bewildering range of interests and attitudes to their subject. As a very broad generalisation I would say that there are discernible within the ranks of sociologists two types of people. One type takes a sociological phenomenon which does not, on the face of it, appear to be too complex, but by dressing it up in difficult words and concepts, manages to make it a major problem for understanding: this type I call 'the complicator'. The other type of sociologist accepts that society is complicated enough already and sees his task as being that of trying to simplify the complex structure so as to increase understanding of it. This type I call 'the simplifier' and I make no bones about being more in sympathy with him than with the other type.

It may then be that to some readers this book may seem oversimple in places. If this is so, the reader may refer to the bibliography where I recommend a number of more advanced works, many of which will be at least twice as long as this volume. I have tried to write an introduction to sociological enquiry which will make the reader aware of the problems and pitfalls of sociological enquiry, but which will not, I hope, deter him from trying his hand. In this book I have also tried hard to avoid the formality (and even pompousness) which characterises quite a lot of sociological writing. If some of my jokes misfire, or if you have heard them before, 'don't shoot the pianist, he is doing his best'.

I would like to thank Dr. Bryan Wilson, the editor of this series, for his encouragement and advice in the writing of this book. His encouragement has always been accepted, his advice not always, and so I accept fully any blame for faults. I would also like to thank Mrs. Margaret Sayles of the Sociology Department of Sheffield University for seeing the manuscript through to the completed typescript. Few authors can be as fortunate as I am in having secretarial assistance of her quality. Finally, to uncounted numbers of students who have taught me how to teach I acknowledge my unpayable debt.

Peter H. Mann
Sheffield University.

1

Sociology and Science

Sociology, as one of the social sciences, is concerned with the behaviour of human beings in society. Other social sciences, such as economics or politics, are also concerned with man's social behaviour. We need to begin, therefore, by considering in what ways sociology differs from other social sciences in its subject matter. Morris Ginsberg once wrote that, 'In the broadest sense, sociology is the study of human interactions and interrelations, their conditions and consequences.'[1] There are dozens of different definitions of sociology (indeed each writer of a text book usually concocts one as a matter of course) but Ginsberg's definition will suffice as a starting point.

Sociology is concerned with the conditions and consequences of social interaction and interrelationships. It is therefore concerned with the structure of society and the effects on social life of certain structures. Sociology deals greatly with group life, and treats with groups as groups—from small family groups to whole societies. We are all of us members of groups, dozens and dozens of groups of all kinds. We may not think this is so if we limit our concept of group membership to such obvious ones as our family, our workplace, our church, our tennis club or our political party. But if we widen the idea of group to cover membership of trades-unions, insurance companies, holders of driving-licences, rate-payers and football-pool 'investors', then we find ourselves members of an almost limitless number of groups. It may be felt that to use the word 'group' to encompass such social aggregations as the family and trades-unions under one heading is to stretch one word too wide for it to be useful. This is a valid point, and sociology seeks to devise new concepts to describe better forms of social interaction which have important points of difference as well as certain similarities. Thus we find the

[1] M. Ginsberg: *Sociology*, Oxford University Press, 1934, p. 8.

terms primary and secondary groups as long-established differentiating concepts, and sociological typologists such as Talcott Parsons have created very complex forms of antithetical descriptions of this sort.

Social interaction, then, with the social structures which accompany it in its many manifestations, is an exceedingly complex field for study. And to claim for sociology that it is a *scientific* study of society, would seem to be claiming too much. No sensible sociologist would deny that to attempt to study scientifically the society in which he lives is difficult. Not only is the field for study extraordinarily complicated, but also the sociologist is a part of it himself, with all his personal values, biases and prejudices.

The difficulty is to know where to start on a truly scientific approach, and, sad to relate, some people never bother and are happy to put forward their own highly-biased views as sociological 'findings'. This is both misleading and at times mischievous, and does the subject great harm. It will be a constant theme of this book that personal bias in sociology must be eradicated as far as is humanly possible.

Where then to start on this difficult task? Some critics of sociology have claimed that it is a study of the obvious. This line of argument usually follows the theme that we are all of us members of society, we live our lives in society, and to do so we must be able to understand it. Why then is there a need for this pretentious nonsense called sociology which only wraps up in fancy words statements of things we all know full well already? Jargon can make any simple statement look very erudite until one strips away the verbiage, and to these critics sociology appears to be only common sense made to look difficult.

On the other hand, there are people who feel that sociology is wasting its time trying to explain the unexplainable. Human motivations and behaviour patterns appear far too complicated for scientific generalisations. If sociologists really knew anything which could be used for the good of society, why is our crime-rate rising all the time? Why do they not get to the root causes of race riots and wildcat strikes and stop them? This particular line of criticism often points to the uniqueness of social events and indicates how terribly complex are all the factors which operate in even the simplest social situation. How then can sociologists hope to 'explain' social behaviour; even less to predict or control it?

Obviously both of these criticisms, although they come from almost diametrically opposite angles, contain some valid points, but they are also criticisms which sociology must refute if it is to be accepted as a scientific discipline. Simple points can be raised at once to some of the critics—to those who claim that sociology is all so obvious it could be said that we certainly do all live in societies, but how many of us have any systematic understanding of their workings? To take one simple case, British society has certain forms of social stratification but who would have the courage to claim that we all of us understand how our social class system works? As individuals we participate personally in only a minute segment of the total social life of our society, and it would be a foolhardy, and indeed stupid, person who claimed that nothing in our society baffled him.

The critics who use the argument of too much complexity are proved wrong every minute of the day. If life were utterly complex it would be unlivable—no one would ever know what to do next or what was likely to happen next. It is the very orderliness of so much of our social life which refutes the complexity criticisms. In breakfasting and coming to work this morning I have myself been enabled to do so by the orderliness of great public utilities such as water and electricity boards which have provided services that I confidently expect to be there each morning. In waiting for the newspaper and the post to arrive I have relied upon certain repeated patterns of behaviour being carried out. And in driving my car from home to university I have, at the peril of serious accident, relied on the other motorists and pedestrians I encountered to keep certain rules of social behaviour just as I have done myself.

These simple examples of patterned behaviour can be used to lead onto the more positive case which will now be made out for the existence of sociology as a scientific discipline.

All social interaction, whether it is just interaction between two people or between thousands of people in highly complex groups, is based upon expectations of behaviour. Any interaction based upon correct expectations means that *prediction* becomes an important part of social life. Not only are we able to predict the actions of individuals (for example, that our own postman, newspaper boy and milkman will deliver their goods to our house) but also we predict the actions of classes or categories of people with whom we have no personal contact at all. Thus in turning on the water tap or the light switch we are making social predictions about hundreds of public utility workers. The utter chaos which results from the failure of such supplies, as in bad winters or cases of strikes, only underlines how confident we are in our ordinary lives about our predictions.

So in our prediction of social behaviour we are, in effect, saying something like this, 'From my knowledge and experience of the society in which I live, I can predict with a fair degree of accuracy that each day the public services will provide us with gas, electricity, water and waste-disposal; that transport services by bus, train, ship and aeroplane will be available for us to go from A to B; that factories, offices, shops and buildings will be open and operating between certain hours.' The list of these predictions can be quite endless the more detailed we become.

In all these predictions it is important to note that we are not concerned with predicting individual behaviour. We do not predict that our neighbour, John Smith, will leave his home at 8.15 to catch the 8.33 train to arrive at his office at 9.15. There will be many John Smiths who, for one reason or another will not do so each day, but we shall be predicting with a high degree of accuracy for hundreds or thousands of people who have not deviated from their normal patterns of everyday behaviour. Our prediction then is essentially a social one, and it is not invalidated by a number of exceptions to it.

Some predictions, of course, are more accurate than others, and it is in the dressing up of rather low-level predictions that sociologists sometimes incur the wrath of the 'commonsense' critics. Nevertheless, there are forms of prediction which can be expressed numerically with quite high degrees of accuracy which are essentially commonsense, yet would never be called pretentious nonsense. Actuarial predictions, for example, use detailed information from the past and present to predict into the future and actuaries are highly skilled, and highly rewarded, men and women working in highly successful organisations. The fact that they can predict accurately and quantitatively makes them extremely useful people. In sickness, accidents and crime we can look to the past and the present and then (probably using a safeguarding clause such as 'other things being equal') we may say that we see no reason why the present trend should not give us such-and-such a figure next year, or even over the next decade. Many people, particularly in such fields as education, health and town-planning, have to make predictions to enable future needs to be met in advance. If these predictions turn out wrong (as unfortunately they do from time to time) then society finds the problems of social adjustment all the more difficult.

But the bulk of the predictions dealt with so far have been of a quantitative nature. One might feel that expectations of deaths on the road or from carcinoma of the lung are of social interest, but hardly at the core of sociology itself. This is true indeed, but it would be foolish not to look beyond quantitative evidence to see the collective attitudes which these figures demonstrate. There is no doubt whatsoever that motor cars could be made much safer than they are today, but motor manufacturers are loath to spend money on safety features, and many motorists are equally uninterested in doing anything for themselves. The latter point is well illustrated by the still small proportion of older cars which are fitted with safety belts, and, of course, the large number of motor-cyclists who do not wear crash-helmets. Lung cancer and smoking have been linked together in carefully conducted statistical surveys, but the tobacco companies are still perfectly respectable enterprises accepting public money for investment in their shares, and are permitted to advertise and sell their goods with very few restrictions. The straightforward quantitative facts about deaths from these two particular causes may be said to throw an interesting light on social attitudes towards 'freedom to die' in a society which places great emphasis on the prolongation of life and will provide extensive medical facilities for people *after* they have been maimed or have acquired lung cancer. Basic statistics, therefore, are of great value to the sociologist in helping him to build up his understanding of society on a firm foundation.

But accidents and ill-health are probably of less interest to the sociologist than are aspects of what is sometimes called 'social pathology.' In Britain particularly, poverty has always interested social investigators, as have crime and delinquency. These are fields of social behaviour where the social values of our society lead us to wish to eradicate such instances. But as soon as we turn to the field of *social* pathology an immediate problem of definitions arises. In medical statistics a death is fairly easily defined, and instances of accidents or diseases can be classified and categorised without too much difficulty since there is general agreement on the definitions (i.e. diagnoses). But how does one define poverty? Crime would seem to be an easier problem of definition since there are annual statistics presented by the Home Office using terms which seem quite clear. But here again the picture can be too simple. Do the terms used today mean the same thing as they meant twenty years ago? Have new categories of offences been created which make it look as if other offences have declined? What is a crime anyway? Is it one 'known to the police', or one in which a charge was laid, or was it one in which the person accused was found guilty? As soon as we start asking questions such as these we are reminded that the most successful crimes are those which are never discovered. And we may well note that the police use a great deal of discretion in the prosecutions they make; a sudden increase, for example, in prosecutions for soliciting for homosexual purposes in a police area is probably indicative of a directive from the chief constable to his staff rather than an increase in the offences themselves.

These sorts of problems only emphasise the difficulties to be overcome in sociology in formulating clear concepts and in measuring the incidence of certain types of social behaviour. Where standardisation of definition is achieved then instances can be gathered together for analysis, and, with varying degrees of accuracy, predictions may be made. The statistical projection over time is the most commonplace of this type.

But now to consider another type of prediction. You, the reader, are asked to close your eyes and conjure up a mental picture of the inside of a prison, with the prisoners queueing up for a meal. Do this now.

Did you manage that? And did you imagine those prisoners to be men or women? I have tried this experiment with students for years and I have yet to find the student—even with half the class girls—

who thinks of women prisoners. Apart from the satisfaction it gives me to predict so accurately each year, this little example shows how we tend to associate one phenomenon with another. Approximately ninety per cent of criminals *are* men anyway, so it is not surprising that we tend to association masculinity with criminality. And we would be on a fairly safe wicket to predict that in the coming year about nine out of ten criminals will be men. If it turned out the other way round we would all be very surprised indeed.

This simple example, linking masculinity with criminality, demonstrates an important aspect of social prediction. The linking together of characteristics is an important part of social investigation, and it has a long, and at times humorous, history. There is the famous correlation between the stipends of curates and the cost of rum in the West Indies which links up two factors which can hardly stand in any causal relationship to each other. I once heard an undergraduate in a debate put forward the claim that the divorce rate amongst people who kept pet giraffes was very low, and the keeping of pet giraffes should therefore be encouraged by all those who hold dear the sanctity of married life. But these ridiculous examples only highlight the importance of the real links between social phenomena. We shall not deal here with the logical aspects of causal relationships, or the spurious correlations which can be demonstrated in statistical studies; these are dealt with adequately in any number of books. Our purpose here is to concentrate on sociological links between variables.

A good example can be seen in the case of criminal behaviour and other characteristics. In the nineteenth century Lombroso put forward an interesting, though untenable, set of 'criminal' physical characteristics. Although this charming linkage could not be upheld we still hear people say of a man that 'he looks a real crook', although this is much more likely to stem from the physical types favoured by comics and films than any other source. In a series of articles on crime in a Sunday newspaper a few years ago, a member of parliament, Mr. Christopher Mayhew, suggested that criminals suffered from 'emotional immaturity'. This would be an interesting link if anyone could establish what emotional immaturity is.

Nevertheless, as can be seen from these examples, factor A may be linked with factor B in some way if only we could define clearly what A and B are in clearly observable terms. Lombroso's physical characteristics were clearly set out. Mayhew's concept was almost wholly undefined.

Montesquieu attempted to link social and psychological traits with various areas of the world, and this type of linkage still tends to exist in various ways today. Montesquieu thought of northern people in Europe as being tough and hardy because of the constant battle with their climate, and people south of the Mediterranean rather soft because of the warm climate, and we in Britain today find it hard to rid ourselves of stereotypes of hardy Scots and soft-living southerners, even though central heating and decent clothing can combat most climatic rigours. Other common linkages in this stereotype category would include the linkage of Scots with meanness, Welsh with musical qualities, Irish with fecklessness and so on. These links may be useful to music-hall comedians, but for sociology they are largely untenable suppositions.

In serious sociology there are more likely to be attempts to link juvenile delinquency with broken homes, academic attainment with social class, and political stability with democratic government. Some linkages may be on a very large scale indeed—even at the level of whole societies. Work of this nature tends to be very speculative and closely associated with historical analysis and usually particularly concerned with the state. For example, when Karl Marx was making his predictions about the future of the class struggle it is difficult to say whether he was mainly a historian, a political theorist, or a sociologist. Some contemporary sociologists are still greatly influenced by Marx. In his case, and that of such modern sociologists, the desire for great social change comes before that of objective analysis.

Linkages, then, may be sought at all sorts of levels of study, from problem families through to problem societies, and some links may turn out to be more useful than others. Note that we are being very cautious here in terminology and not saying correlations, which suggest statistical links, and certainly not causal relationships which mean that A is actually caused by B. Even in the physical sciences, where research is far more advanced than in the social sciences, researchers are very wary of claiming that one thing causes another. We may be able, in science, to say *how* things happen, but it is usually left to the theologians to say *why*.

But if we can, no matter how crudely, link social characteristics together, where do we go from there? We may be able to predict that a larger proportion of children from middle class homes will pass the 11+ examination (where it still exists) compared with children from working class homes. This may be an interesting piece of information, but what good is it to anyone? This particular example is a useful one to use as a peg for discussing the differences between pure and applied research.

Whilst the division between the two is a matter of degree and not a simple dichotomy, it could be said that the pure scientist derives his greatest satisfaction from increasing his knowledge in a field of enquiry where many questions remain unanswered. To him the challenge of not knowing is paramount. If he can solve the problem he is satisfied, and the results may or may not have any practical use. The pure scientist would probably argue that knowledge itself is always of practical use in the end, if only in opening our minds wider. The more applied scientist would tend to begin by seeing his research in a practical context from the onset. He would regard a sociological 'problem' as one in which action could be taken to 'improve' matters. The applied scientist is therefore much more likely to be working within a certain set of values, although these may not be those of his own society (e.g. the Marxist oriented sociologist who actively wishes to change his society.)

It is doubtful if many 'applied' sociologists would be interested in studying the declining power of the British aristocracy, since they would merely note this was a fact and probably applaud it. But a truly 'pure' researcher could well find the aristocracy a most interesting field of enquiry and one which has been 'gone over' much less than the middle or working classes.

From time to time particular areas of study seem to have a vogue. At one time it might be juvenile delinquency, at another time old people and their problems, at yet another teenagers and their morals. All these fields could be studied just to find out; on the other hand they could be studied with a view to reducing delinquency, helping

B

old people or improving adolescent morals. All these motives imply a desire for social change, a desire to predict so that some form of control can be exerted so as to bring about a change.

To return, then, to the 11+ and social class. The pure sociologist might be attracted to this question because the initial relationship between success in the examination and parental social class seemed to throw up even more questions. Why should there be this link? What deeper forces are operating here? Do the examiners favour middle class children? Obviously they do not since social class does not come into the examination. Why then do the middle class children do better? Are they really more intelligent? What do we mean by intelligent? Do the primary school teachers favour middle class children and help them more? Does social class come into streaming selection? Do streamed children do better than unstreamed ones? Are middle class children more literate and numerate than working class ones? Do homes where parents actually own and read books influence children? Does parental interest in school work help or hinder children? Is a heavy diet of television compatible with school success? These and a host of other questions suggest themselves from this particular question simply because it is obvious that the examination success is not just simply caused by social class; this is only a convenient shorthand symbol to describe all sorts of social differences which exist between people. To keep on digging away at these layers is challenge enough to the pure scientist.

For the applied scientist, though, this would not suffice. The current interest in education and social class commends itself to many sociologists because they see in it examples of what might be called social injustice. Several studies have shown that working class children do not do as well, intelligence for intelligence, as do their middle class counterparts. If this is so our society is loosing good potential and this is a social problem to be solved. Irrespective of egalitarian principles which may motivate some researchers, others less biased see education as a social organisation which stands in need of improvement if the best is to be gained both for and from all ranges of ability among young people. The applied scientist then is working on the same data as the pure scientist, but whilst the latter would perhaps stop short of advocating changes, the applied scientist is prepared to step in and say what could be done to 'improve' the situation.

Whilst it may be difficult enough for the pure scientist to eliminate value judgments and keep himself from getting entangled in the 'oughts' of living, the applied scientist has a much greater problem of maintaining his scientific position. Once he starts to indicate what ought to be done he is stepping outside the structure of scientific investigation and is becoming a moral human being, with no more credentials for saying what should be done than anyone else.

Here the problem arises for the applied scientist of disentangling his predictions from his predilections. An applied scientist could well work on the problem of educational selection at 11 (or any other age) with a view to helping in the making of policy which would increase the use of young people's academic potential. But to act as a scientist in this context he must use the values put forward as facts. Thus he must, in effect, say to the policy makers 'You tell me what ends you want to achieve and I will do my best to tell you how you can best achieve them. I may not, as a private person, agree with your ends, but I can, as a scientist, tell you how best to work for them'. If, though, the researcher says 'I think that society should work for certain ends and I am going to try to find out how these ends can best be achieved' then he forfeits his status as a scientist because of the first part of this sentence, although he may still work as a scientist on the latter part. The matter is, of course, more complicated than this since there are some people who might carry out highly selective research only looking for the favourable evidence, supporting their values and ignoring contrary evidence, and there could be people who do not even carry out scientific enquiries, but try to garnish highly suspect studies with perhaps a few technical words, or even a few statistical tests, to make spurious work look like genuine sociology.

There are, then, many reasons why sociology is viewed with suspicion, especially by natural scientists who feel that the objectivity and impartiality of the sciences is endangered by this young and, at present, highly popular subject. Atomic physicists may have qualms of conscience about the use made of their discoveries by government establishments, but the physicist who is a member of C.N.D. stands in the latter position just as a human being—he does not claim any special expertise over his fellow members about knowing the right course for mankind. The problem with the sociologist is that he has to work with data which are likely to stir his conscience and to involve him in matters of conscience in a highly complex way. Indeed, the very speciality within sociology (e.g. political or educational sociology) may have attracted the researcher in the first place because this is a field of social behaviour about which he has strong feelings. In race relations especially we have a field of enquiry where I know of no sociologist or anthropologist concerned who does not feel strongly against the inequalities which result from social segregation. An apartheid-supporting race relations specialist in sociology or anthropology in Britain would be regarded as a freak.

In all the discussion so far the reader will have noticed that the word scientist has been used a great deal, even where at times it might be thought that the claims of sociologists to be scientists appear to be slightly suspect. Before going any further, therefore, it is important to clarify just what is meant by this term 'science' and so, in the following chapter, particular attention will be focused on the concept of science itself.

So far we have discussed in general terms the problem of sociology as a science. Now we shall look in detail at science itself, so that we can then move on to consider the application of scientific method to the study of social phenomena.

2

Scientific Method in Sociology

Even today when, as politicians never tire of telling us, we live in an age of science and technology, there is still something of an aura of mystery surrounding the idea of 'science'. Perhaps led on by comic-strips and science fiction, people think of scientists and science as something apart from the ordinary run of everyday life. At a time when mankind is beset by problems of over-population we look to 'science' to solve the problems of starvation in 'under-developed' countries. As the diseases of civilisation, such as cancer and cardiac diseases, take a greater toll each year, we look to 'science' for the answers.

This conception of science is almost inextricably bound up with mental pictures of men in white coats (perhaps with more hair on their chins than their crowns) boiling up strange liquids in complex glass apparatus, or pressing rows and rows of buttons as wiggly electric lines shoot across squared screens. The interior of Dr. Who's space ship is a perfect example of this stereotype of science, and it tends to lead the uninitiated into thinking of science as all bubbles and squiggles.

It will be our concern in this chapter to make two fundamental points against this conception of science. Firstly, it will be explained that science is better defined in terms of method than subject matter under study. And secondly it will be shown that science is a matter of degree rather than an absolute 'is' or 'is not'.

Taking the first point of method and subject matter, it can be seen that a definition of a science according to the phenomena studied is difficult to maintain with any sense of uniformity. If we think of 'subjects' such as physics and chemistry as sciences, do we think of botany and zoology as sciences also? Or do we somehow feel that botany and zoology, whilst being sciences, are not quite as scientific as physics and chemistry? It may well be that many of us have made some such sort of distinction for a long time, but when we come to look at this question the distinction is not easy to explain. But the subject matters of botany and zoology are plants and animals, and many famous artists have painted flowers and horses. Does this make these artists scientists then? After all, they are dealing with the subject matter of botany and zoology. Yet it is doubtful if one would say of van Gogh's painting of the Sunflower, or one of Stubb's paintings of a race-horse, 'Ah, there is the work of a true scientist!'

Apart from this sort of problem, there is the question of how one categorises the newly grown so-called 'social' sciences. They deal with people and their activities, so we have to sort out which subjects dealing with people are sciences and which are not. Psychology, sociology, economics and politics are generally considered to be social sciences. But history is usually considered an 'arts' subject, whilst geography may well be classified as arts, science or social science according to where it happens to be found in an academic syllabus. And literature abounds with the study of human behaviour, but English is probably never referred to as a science.

So in trying to label subjects science or not, according to subject matter, the position rapidly becomes very muddled and that is why it is better to use another sort of classification—by considering the *way* in which subjects are studied. If we can agree that a certain *method* is indicative of science we can then agree to call a study scientific if this method is used. And if, instead of just saying that some fields of enquiry are scientific and others are not, we agree that some may be *more* scientific than others, because of the sophistication of the method used, then we will have employed the second part of the definition of science also.

Let us be quite clear that this form of description does not do away completely with problems of nomenclature, since many people may be working in a certain field using different methods. Thus a person who studies society using scientific method we would call a true sociologist and therefore a scientist. A person recording impressions of society, but being highly subjective about it, as might be a reporter or a book-writing traveller, would be neither sociologist nor scientist, valuable and illuminating though his work might be.

All this adds up to the fact that it is possible to carry out scientific work in any field at all so long as scientific method is being used. If we accept this then it is clearly possible for a person to make a scientific study of religion so long as scientific method is used. It is possible to study Shakespeare's sonnets scientifically so long as scientific method is used. And equally it is possible to make an unscientific study of human behaviour when scientific method is not used.

The important thing is now to define what is meant by scientific method, and the classic statement by the British scientist Karl Pearson cannot be bettered. Pearson said, 'The man who classifies facts of any kind whatever, who sees their mutual relation and describes their sequences, is applying the scientific method and is a man of science. . . . When every fact . . . has been examined, classified and co-ordinated with the rest, then the mission of science will be completed.'[1] To qualify as the scientific study of social behaviour sociology must observe systematically, classify systematically and interpret systematically. The better it does these three things the more it can claim to be a science. It will, therefore, be valuable next to consider the three fundamental processes of observation, classification and interpretation separately and in some detail.

Observation

We all observe, but we rarely observe systematically. In social observation we deal mainly with things that we see and hear. All of us with normal sight and hearing respond in a very similar way to sights and sounds, so it might seem that observation presents few problems. It is obviously very difficult to observe meaningfully a ceremony carried out in a culture foreign to our own where a language we do not understand is used, but even here we could observe what actions take place. But could we?

Even in the simplest social situation it is impossible to describe the *totality* of the actions which take place. Let us take as an example a highly ritualised social situation such as a wedding service in an Anglican church. The 'order' of the service and the words to be used

[1] Karl Pearson: *The Grammar of Science*, London, 1900, pp. 12–13.

are all set down in the prayer-book, so that the basic outlines are
clearly set out for the observer. But suppose that twenty different
observers were given the task of reporting in full everything which
they saw or heard at a wedding. Would we really expect them all to
turn in identical reports? The answer is surely no. Apart from the
fact that a *complete* report would be enormous in its length the
observer would find it impossible to see or hear all that was going on
at any instant of time and he would be hard pressed, even with shorthand or a tape recorder, to record everything he saw or heard. The
totality of the situation would, strictly speaking, include not only the
physical descriptions of every person present and the clothes they
wore, but also every small movement they made or word they
whispered during the service. Obviously observation of a *total* situation is neither feasible nor is it likely to be of any particular use to
anyone. The point is that we observe situations for a purpose. In the
case of the newspaper reporter at a wedding the purpose is usually
to report on the demeanour of the bride and groom, with some
descriptions of the clothes worn by certain females and perhaps the
behaviour of young attendants if there are any. Wedding reporting
in local newspapers is so highly stereotyped that it is not necessary
for a reporter to be present at all if the people concerned are prepared
to fill in a standard questionnaire. But I recall in 1947 seeing one
bride and groom coming out from the service where the local newspaper reporter had left out an interesting facet of information. The
groom was a German ex-prisoner of war and the newspaper report
made much of this happy union being forged between two countries
who had so recently been at war and so on. The fact that the bride
was clearly pregnant was not mentioned in the newspaper.

This particular example shows how we may observe certain things,
yet do nothing with the observations. The newspaper reporter did
not include observations on bridal pregnancy amongst the features
he was expected to report on: his observation was selective according
to certain rules of local newspaper reporting. The point is then that
observation *is* normally purposive. There is an old definition of a
psychologist as a person who goes to a strip-show and observes the
audience. In some cases this may well be far more interesting but it is
unusually selective observation.

The principal criterion guiding our observations in a social situation is that of relevance. We normally extract from a total situation those features which are relevant to our interest in the situation. This point was brought home to me once in a case where I saw a young boy, about twelve years old, acting rather strangely in a quiet private road when there was no apparent reason for him being there at all. I was at the time in my car and I was able to move my rear-view mirror so as to get a good view of the boy. Later on a boy was found sleeping in a caravan parked in the private road and the police were informed, since he ran away immediately he was found. I was able to help the police in giving them quite a good description of his facial features, hair, build and so on, and I was quietly complimenting myself on my careful observation until the policeman said, 'And was he wearing long trousers or short trousers?' I had not the faintest idea. My observation had been concentrated so much on the boy from the neck up that I could not honestly say whether he was wearing any trousers at all.

Many psychological experiments on observation show clearly how very selective we are in our observation, and also, of course, how often we see what we want to see or what we expect to see. Conjurors are able to capitalise on these forms of observation in their sleight of hand, and many ardent football fans suffer from distorted observation so far as fouls and offsides are concerned, hence the gratuitous offers of aids to observation for the referee who is appointed as an impartial observer.

In working towards systematic observation it is important to see what is there and not to see things that are not there. The difficulty is that any social situation is so complex that in selecting the features that we observe we are always in danger of leaving out important factors which are of unsuspected relevance. We shall discuss this in more detail later, but for the moment it will suffice to note that if we were observing the behaviour of students at a dance we would automatically register the sex of each person we watched (that is assuming that sex was distinguishable by simple observation). But we would probably ignore the colour of their hair or of their eyes, or the fact that some were left-handed and some right-handed because we would pre-suppose that these factors had no relevance to the social interaction taking place. But if some of the students had black skins we would probably note this fact quite specifically since we would probably expect colour of skin to have some link with social interaction. Of course, the fact of hair colour *could* be noted in our observations if we felt that the old saying that gentlemen prefer blondes had any veracity. Our selectivity of observation will be according to what we think is relevant and what is not relevant to our particular interest at the time. If a very old tune were to be played at the dance, perhaps the young man might croon into his partner's ear that 'I only have eyes for you', which would indicate a highly, even dangerous, selective limitation on his observation of the total situation.

But whilst we may recognise the problems of observation in a total situation there is a further problem of communicating what we see to other people. This leads us on to our next aspect of scientific enquiry.

Classification

Classification is essentially a form of putting together things which have certain similarities so as to be able to deal with them more easily. Very often this 'dealing with' them is bound up with communicating our observations to other people.

Very early in their lives young children learn to classify and communicate their observations. At times this can be amusing, or even embarrassing, as when a very young child observes an adult male and classifies him under the category 'daddy' and calls this out loudly in public. This fairly commonplace event is simply an example of observation which is correct in noting sex and age, but wrong in selection of other factors, such as facial features, clothes, and so on, and thus also wrong in kinship position.

The old game of 'Animal, Mineral, Vegetable', perhaps better known through the mass media as '20 Questions' is a good example of locating the individual item by a process of gradual classification into smaller and smaller categories. The game begins with the largest categories and gradually fines down to the smallest, using a simple dichotomous, yes-no, method.

The whole process of classification is a way of grouping together objects, actions, attitudes, beliefs—all sorts of phenomena which are needed to be collected together to help understand a complex situation. In the football crowd instanced previously, we would be classifying those people present if we referred to them as men / women, men/boys, home team supporters/visitors' supporters, season-ticket holders/pay-at-the-gate supporters, and so on. Classification helps to make sense of the whole scene by reducing innumerable similar types to classes which can be handled by the observer.

A simple example is to be found in statistical classification, which is often the first thing dealt with in a text book on statistics. To describe an individual person according to sex, age, height and weight is not difficult: to do this individually for a hundred people would be tedious in the extreme, and as a description of the group of 100 people would be quite useless, since the listener or reader would be quite bewildered by the end of it all. So to convey to the reader the general picture of the group we classify our subjects according to certain categories which are useful to us at the time. Sex is simple—just male or female. Age could be any form of classification we want at the time: it might, for legal purposes, be only 'under 21' and 'adult'. It might differentiate people by 10-year groups (e.g. 20–29, 30–39 and so on) or it might particularly note pensioners as being 65 or over. Whatever classifications we use, and the same would apply for height and weight, we are putting people together in bundles so that we can, at the cost of losing certain individual details, get a better picture of the group as a group.

But whilst some phenomena, such as sex or age, are fairly easy to classify, other features are not so easy. A variable such as sex is, in statistics, called 'discrete' because, simply put, there are no problems about the boundaries. You are either a male or a female—there are no degrees about this classification and the criteria we use for deciding what is male and what is female are universally agreed ones. The variable of age is statistically called a 'continuous' one, since the shades of age can be almost infinitely measured. We find that for many purposes age in complete years since birth is adequate classification, but obviously we could go into more detail and classify by months, weeks, days or even hours, minutes and seconds. But these latter classes would be so numerous that they would not usually be of much use to anyone.

Nevertheless, one can see that in classifying even continuous variables such as age, height and weight, the features to be classified are generally agreed on. The measuring scales may differ; we might measure height and weight in metric units rather than inches or pounds, but on the whole we are not in trouble about *what* we are measuring. When it comes to classifying social factors the problems become much more difficult. An obvious example in sociology is that factor of social differentiation in hierarchical fashion which we sometimes call social class. How do we classify people in this particular way? It is not easy, because the factors we are dealing with are so much less easy to observe. We shall have more to say later about problems of specifically sociological classification, but we may note here that although we are accustomed to measuring physical objects such as lengths of cloth or electric flex in inches, feet and yards, there is nothing mystical or God-given about these units. We respond to the concept of length in a particular way which is useful because we have all agreed what inches, feet and yards mean, and we have measuring tools which are all the same. So if I buy a yard of electric cord at a shop it is still a yard when I get it home because the shopkeeper and I have both used the same measures.[2] But we could just as well have measured the flex in metres or decimetres; it is simply a cultural fact that we agreed on feet and inches.

Agreement is not so easy in sociological phenomena. So often we are dealing with intangibles such as community feeling, educational opportunity and bureaucratic organisation. To classify social interaction and structure so that we all agree what we are talking about is a very difficult task indeed. And the answer is not just simply to quantify everything and turn it into numbers, since in the act of measuring a phenomenon with very elaborate measuring indices we may be in danger of losing sight of the more basic problems; that is, to copy a little from Wilde, we may have the measure of everything, but the relevance of nothing. Some critics of the

---

[2] See Dorothy Davis: *A History of Shopping*, London, 1966, for examples of lack of standardisation in the eighteenth and nineteenth centuries.

elaborate American techniques of statistical method which have been evolved (especially C. Wright Mills)[3] have expressed doubts about the value of highly complex measuring devices which seem to have become virtually ends in themselves rather than intermediary tools leading towards true sociological understanding. And true sociological understanding is particularly the concern of our third factor—generalisation.

Generalisation

One so often hears people in everyday conversation say, often about social phenomena, 'But, of course, it's very difficult to generalise'. And indeed it is. But sociology, as a science, is concerned with working towards generalisations.

Let us suppose that we are interested in the problems of juvenile delinquency in this country. As scientists we want to try to link delinquency with other observable factors so that we can understand better the background and (sticking our necks out) the 'causes' of delinquency. What use may be made of our findings we will, at this stage, leave to one side. The work we shall attempt in this field of enquiry will be that of finding what other traceable factors go along with this behaviour which we have classified as delinquency. If we take one particular case of a boy, let us call him Kevin, we may find that certain features in his background and history seem, on the face of things, to have some link with his appearance in the juvenile court and subsequent conviction. His father died when Kevin was a baby. His mother has had a series of 'lodgers' ever since then. Kevin's elder brother graduated from approved school, via Borstal, to adult prison. Kevin's home is a two-roomed apartment with no separate kitchen or bathroom, in the heart of a slum district. Kevin himself is below average intelligence (though no moron) and has a record of truancy from the local comprehensive school which he attends. A description such as this, which is entirely fictitious, probably has us nodding our heads and saying mentally, 'Yes, that's just what you would expect.' Why do we accept this sort of evidence as being something that satisfies us in our need for explanation? If we

[3] C. Wright Mills: *The Sociological Imagination*, Oxford University Press, 1959.

had been told that Kevin was dark-haired, blue-eyed, right-handed and blood-group O we would have been puzzled as to the relevance of this list of factors. The essential point here is that Kevin's background fits in with what has already been established about delinquents—Kevin is a particular case who fits in with the generalisations already made from previous studies. And the generalisations already made are, of course, derived from dozens, hundreds or thousands of studies of people like him.

Perhaps this all sounds rather too easy, and Kevin's deplorable social background makes him the sort of case who sounds like a boy doomed to delinquency by his environmental factors. But to complicate the issue we find that there are hundreds of boys with many of the features that go with Kevin who have never been delinquent in their lives; fine, upstanding boys from broken families, living in deplorable slum houses, helping their mothers and being a joy to everyone. On the other hand, right after Kevin's case is dealt with, we have an almost identical offence committed by Giles, the carefully brought-up son of a professional man, educated at a private school, living in a lovely house in a select suburb with no 'problems' one could ever think of. Where does Giles fit into our generalisation?

This is where we find ourselves saying that, after all, a generalisation is only a generalisation, and we would always expect there to be exceptions. We might even go so far as to say that it is the exceptions which prove the rule—though here the word 'prove' actually means 'test'. The important point about generalisations, especially in the social sciences, is that they are only probability statements, not statements of absolute certainty. Without going into a discussion of formal logic let us accept that if you cut off a person's head all evidence that we have ever had shows that the person will die. Cause and effect stand in a clear relationship to each other. Similarly in physics we learn very early on that if we heat a steel ball it always expands. In chemistry we learn that sulphur trioxide passed through water always gives us sulphuric acid. We say 'always' because under the normal experimental conditions these results always do occur. But in sociology broken homes do not always produce delinquency; indeed only a minority of broken homes, thank goodness, produce delinquents. But looked at the other way round quite a lot of delinquents come from broken homes. The value of this linkage is to indicate to us that if we have a delinquent we are likely to find in the background some evidence of family breakdown. We cannot always expect to be able to do anything to remedy the background, this is a matter of social policy not sociology, but we are, by establishing generalisations, helping ourselves in deciding what to look *for* in individual cases.

In sociology we are concerned with situations in which we shall be content to say that under stipulated circumstances condition A is more likely to be linked with factor Y than with Z. It is of the nature of complex sociological situations that there are likely to be many more factors operating than just Y, and in this we are faced with the problems of multiple causation in social behaviour. But at this point it suffices to recognise that sociology is concerned with probabilities, not certainties. The good sociologist could well take as his motto for research the saying of Benjamin Franklin that the only certainties are death and taxes.

The fact that one cannot make absolutely definite claims to causal links between factors does not in any way detract from the claims of sociology to be a science. Most sciences today are concerned with probabilities rather than certainties although in some of the natural sciences it has only been with the greater development of knowledge that the work has become so refined that scientists have come to realise their own ignorance. If this sounds rather 'Irish', an explanation may help us to see a further problem in sociology, that of the refinement of concepts. If you are trying to explain what happens in a physical situation you have to use some concepts or other to describe the phenomena under study. In physics we find that the concept of the molecule was useful in the explanation of physical behaviour. But the molecule only answered the questions satisfactorily so long as the questions asked were not too detailed. But when some questions were asked as a result of increasing knowledge the concept of the molecule became inadequate and, to shorten a long story, we have gradually refined our concepts from molecules to atoms to particles and so on. Put simply we might say that 'Ask a crude question and a crude concept will do for the answer'. But once this answer has been given the scientist will come back again and ask for a slightly less crude answer, because some point of detail no longer satisfies him.

In sociology this sort of process of coming back is only in its infancy, but it is of the very essence of scientific enquiry. If we say that juvenile delinquency is associated with broken homes then the true scientist comes back and asks, 'Do you mean all forms of juvenile delinquency?' 'How are you defining the concept of delinquency?' 'Are you using examples of delinquency from America, and if so does the term mean the same as it would do in this country?' 'How are you defining this concept of broken homes?' 'Are you lumping together homes where one parent died with homes where one parent left when the two should really be considered separately?' All these sorts of questions demonstrate clearly how scientific enquiry always throws up more questions than it answers because the very fact of knowing at a lower level stimulates the researchers to want to know at a higher one—that is a more detailed one.

This sort of endless questioning of the present level of knowledge and the pursuit of more detailed understanding of what must be more limited fields of enquiry can be seen in the increasing specialisation necessary in scientific enquiry if really and truly scientific knowledge is to be gained. The day of the all-knowing 'general' scientist is long past in the physical sciences, and it is practically past in the social sciences also. The sociologist today who has not specialised in his research is likely to be a generaliser at a very low level of scientific quality.

The true scientist today then, as the old tag said, 'knows more and more about less and less'; only the second part that 'he eventually ends up knowing everything about nothing' is taking things just a bit too far. But to know more and more about less and less is indicative of the increase in scientific knowledge, since this demonstrates the development of knowledge from crude beginning generalisations to detailed, highly specific generalisations in carefully selected fields of enquiry. What the old tag leaves out is the tremendous growth of science and scientists over the past three centuries. The first known scientific journal, *The Philosophical Transactions of the Royal Society of London* was published in 1665. By 1900 there were 10,000 scientific journals, and today there are getting on for 100,000 such publications. Against such figures the rapid development, and therefore specialisation, of scientific enquiry is easily understandable.[4]

Science is a continuous process of accumulating knowledge and as it expands it inevitably becomes more detailed. Our observations and classifications, our descriptions of social structures and social processes, will become more detailed and more sophisticated. Our generalisations, from earlier somewhat crude and low-level statements applying to somewhat ill-defined concepts will become more numerous as they are more specifically related to clearly defined problem areas in sociology and the generalisations will be more sophisticated for these reasons. The history of sociology itself clearly shows this trend, from the earlier days when sociological generalisations were pitched at the level of whole societies, to the present day where such wide but low-level generalisations are almost wholly eschewed as being too crude to be fruitful.

Operational Definitions

In our sociological observations and classifications we have seen the problem of gaining agreement on how to describe social phenomena. Suppose we want to enquire into social behaviour in a residential area and we have an idea that this is affected by the general positions people hold in society. We may phrase this sociologically by the use of shorter concepts such as 'neighbourhood interaction' being affected by 'social class'. We might even carry out research and end up with a generalisation that neighbourhood interaction is conditioned by social class, but if we do this our readers will want to know what these terms mean. There are two very good reasons for this. Firstly the reader wants to know in more detail just what these shorthand-type concepts mean and secondly he wants sufficient detail to be given so that he himself could repeat the study in just the same way if he felt it should be replicated. Standardisation of concepts is a basic scientific necessity and in research it can be done by the use of the 'operational definition'.

Perhaps the best reference for research sociology in this section is the writing of George Lundberg, an American sociologist who for

[4] See D. J. de Solla Price: *Science Since Babylon*, Yale University Press, 1961, p. 97.

C

many years has reminded sociologists of the problems of scientific methodology. Our communication of observations is made by the use of words and, as Lundberg says, 'All words are symbolic designations of some behaviour phenomenon to which we respond. It is our response which gives it "meaning". The meaning of anything we respond to is implicit in the response and part of it. We do not respond symbolically to that which has *no* meaning to us. Meaningless things, words or symbols are contradictions in terms; the very fact that we call them meaningless proves that they have *that* meaning, i.e. we so classify them.'

If we are going to use words for scientific purposes we must use them carefully and specifically. 'The ultimate test of the value of a particular term or concept must be its usefulness for the purpose at hand, namely, the description of behaviour so objectively as to be subject to corroboration by other persons.' In his textbook on methodology, *Social Research*, Lundberg gives a full argument which is reproduced almost in its entirety here.

Scientists agree to designate each degree or kind of behaviour which their instruments indicate by specific words or other symbols. These words, so defined, may then be used to build up more complicated words, the definition of which is always reducible to the readings of standardised instruments. . . . Such definitions are called 'operational definitions' . . . (they) are merely definitions which consist as far as possible of words clearly designating performable and observable operations subject to corroboration. . . . Now the degree to which the above criteria can be satisfied varies according to the stage of development which a science has reached. . . . It is not considered, therefore, that other definitions which are only imperfectly, slightly or not at all operational may not be valuable in the early stages of a science, and on the frontiers of well-established sciences. They may be useful as first approximations, pending more mature developments. Highly perfected operational definitions are goals to which we strive, rather than tools to be hoped for or conjured up ready made at the outset of an enquiry.[5]

This quotation is given at some length, because it contains a whole

[5] G. Lundberg: *Social Research*, London, 1948, pp. 88–89.

basis for sociological research. If we are to study concepts such as 'social class' or 'neighbourhood interaction' scientifically we must move on from the ordinary, everyday ill-defined usage of words towards some type of definition which can be used by any number of fellow researchers. For social class we cannot be satisfied with descriptions which refer to social solidarity or consciousness of group membership unless these terms are further defined in a way in which they can be observed and classified. It is no use saying that neighbourhood interaction refers to how well people get on together, unless we know what to look for, or ask for, when this behaviour is being studied.

The operational definition is a good corrective to woolly thinking since it forces us to consider how we can convey to other sociologists the full, observable meaning of what we are dealing with. If our concepts cannot be observed by others then we are well on the way to a mystical, subjective sort of study which by its very method cannot be scientific.

It is not a very great step to see that the operational definition lends itself well to quantitative description rather than qualitative. Numbers, rather than words, are attractive to scientists since they are symbols to which we all respond in a uniform way, and numerical linkages between factors can be expressed by means of formulae and tested in accordance with recognised statistical tests. The clear cut attractions of numerical definition have perhaps led some sociologists to an extreme position in the movement towards the scientific study of society. The desire for quantification is understandable, but it can be a desire which leads the researcher to measurement for its own sake rather than towards understanding. We should always question the actual value of scales and indices for the furtherance of sociological knowledge. The sociologist who becomes obsessed with problems of measurement is in danger of not being able to see the wood for the trees. This is not, in any way, to suggest that sociologists should not try to measure. Far be it from us to suggest that measurement is not one of the most valuable of sociological methods. It is merely that measurement in itself is not enough. Measurement for a purpose—a truly sociological purpose leading to generalisation and theory building—is what must be stressed.

Measurement in the social sciences, as a feature of operational definitions, has probably advanced more in psychology than in the other ones. Scales for the measurement of morale, social adjustment, aptitudes for this or that, are commonplace, apart from the more generally recognised measures of the concept of 'intelligence'. In sociology most attention in measurement has been given to measures of 'social class', although it should be noted that the measure in most common use—that formulated by the Registrar-General—is an almost completely arbitrary one, and is not based upon any empirical research. The measure used by most market research practitioners is one formulated by the Institute of Practitioners in Advertising and the only one based upon research by sociologists (usually called the Hall-Jones scale) has not been widely adopted for general research purposes.[6]

If we find it useful at a given time or for a given research project to decide that we will designate social differences according to a particular scale then we are communicating our information in a clear way to other people, as long as they can check up on the way in which we have made our classifications. The Registrar-General, for his classification of people into classes according to their occupations, makes available a large volume which contains practically every occupation one can think of (this is the source of such exotic occupations as 'sagger makers bottom knockers' so beloved of journalists) and if we want to carry out a study of our own in which a comparison with national or regional distributions of 'social class' would be of value, not only do we have the census tables for the country and practically every town and city in it, but also we have the 'guide' to classification of occupations which tells us what class any occupation should go into if we want to use the same method. Given these two points, the attractiveness of the Registrar-General's classification is apparent, since it has the background data we may need, and it is also published anew every ten years or so (with a five year interval possible if the five year sample census proves successful).

In this example can be seen the attraction of a form of operational definition used on a large scale in this country. This classification

[6] See the Market Research Society report, *Social Class Definition in Market Research*, London, 1963, for a study of scales used.

has its faults of arbitrariness but they are greatly outweighed by its value in enabling sociologists to communicate with each other using terms and concepts which are standard rather than personal. To say that a suburb is very 'high class' is subjective, impossible to corroborate without much more information on what the term means, and not a very scientific way of looking at things. To give the distribution according to the Registrar-General's five categories, noting the preponderance of occupied males in categories 1 and 2 is both more exact and more useful for comparison purposes. To link this with a measure, based upon categorised answers to a questionnaire, which gives a 'measure' of neighbourhood interaction can lead further to a neat statistical test indicating whether or not the relationship between social class and neighbourhood interaction is 'significant'. This sort of research is sometimes decried by sociologists (and others) as being mechanical, meaningless, or any of a variety of derogatory terms. Perhaps so, when one disagrees fundamentally with the classifications used in the measure of social class and the questions asked in the index of neighbourhood interaction. But for the measurers it can always be said that they have been open to scrutiny the whole time; there is nothing mysterious or under-cover about their work and anyone could go along with the same instruments and repeat the study. In effect, the argument for this type of work is that it is trying all the way to conform to principles of scientific method, low level though the concepts may be, and crude though the measures may be. If the critics of this work are to be constructive, rather than merely destructive, then it is up to them to produce something better. The pity is that some of the critics tend to be 'theorists' who have no great record of detailed empirical research of their own. The value of the operational definition is not so much, at the present stage of sociology, that it leads immediately to quantification of data, but that it helps the researchers by agreeing about the terms that are used. If the terms used are openly described without any subjectivity or mystique about them, then people can agree on definitions to be used and get on with the work more usefully. There is nothing magical at all about the operational definition, it is simply a way of stating clearly in observable terms what one is going to talk about and then sticking to those terms throughout the research. If one finds that an operational definition used by a researcher is of value then it can be adopted by other people for their research and in the use of uniform definitions science can only be increased.

The Comprehensiveness of Scientific Enquiry

We may now clarify the position of sociology as a science from the point of view of the application of scientific methodology to the particular subject matter of social behaviour and social structure. We have made it clear that any definition of science should be in terms of *method*. George Lundberg said that all that the term science, as applied to a particular field, comes to mean is a field which has been studied according to certain principles, that is to say, according to scientific method. Lundberg goes on to say, 'If our knowledge of a certain field has been derived according to this method, and if that knowledge is applicable to this field for purposes of prediction (and perhaps control), then that body of knowledge may properly be designated as a science, regardless of the nature of the subject matter. The test of the thoroughness (or success) with which the method has been applied is found in our ability to predict the behaviour of classes of phenomena under given conditions.'[7]

Scientific method, then, is distinguished from non-scientific method in a number of ways. First of all scientific method is distinguished by its motive, in that it aims at the discovery of truth, and truth only. Some writers, such as John Madge,[8] may disagree with this, but it is here held that science is detached from emotional, personal, or purely practical objectives. The aim of science is to attain objectivity, impartiality and unbiased observation, and if these criteria can be met then sociology is becoming more of a science.

Also science is distinguished by its continuity and its comprehensiveness. This means that science is not just a collection or even a rag-bag of individual pieces of research and empirical findings. A science is a connected framework and it is in the building up of theory that a science reaches its maturity. Sociology, therefore, to be considered as a science, will be seen always to be seeking to establish

[7] Lundberg, op. cit., pp. 4–5.
[8] See his *Tools of Social Science*, p. 294.

a connected framework in which generalisations may be related. And the more these generalisations are made one can see the more precise form which the generalisations will take. This leads to the third point, then, of exactitude. In all sciences exactitude is sought in the observations and studies carried out. The description of social phenomena is difficult enough at any time and sociology suffers particularly from the difficulties of attaining exactness in its description and measurement. But, nevertheless, this is a criterion of scientific enquiry and it is therefore a goal to be sought. It may be noted that the discovery of objective truth was particularly commented on by Sidney and Beatrice Webb who themselves were very much concerned with the developments in the methodology of the social sciences, and who themselves were aware of their own extremely strong personal biases about the society in which they lived. The Webbs said, 'Most people, without being aware of it, would much rather retain their own conclusions than learn anything contrary to them. . . . Most beginners do not realise that a good half of most research consists in an attempt to prove yourself wrong. It is a law of the mind that, other things being equal, those facts which seem to bear out his own preconceived view of things will make a deeper impression on the student than those which seem to tell in the opposite direction.'[9] It is difficult to know on what series of findings the Webbs 'law of the mind' was based but nevertheless there is great wisdom in this statement. The sociologist must always try to stand neutrally at the centre of things and he more than any other scientist perhaps must be constantly aware of the dangers of seeing only those things which he wants to see and not seeing those things which appear to tell against his own biases.

In the next chapter we shall look at some of the major problems with which the sociologist is faced in his working towards the development of sociological theory bearing in mind the importance of scientific methodology in his subject.

[9] In *Methods of Social Study*, London, 1932, p. 36.

3

Basic Steps in Sociological Investigation

Some Wrong Ideas on the Concept of Theory

The way in which the word 'theory' is used in everyday speech, and even at times by sociologists, can lead the beginning researcher into some of the most unfortunate errors imaginable. A prevalent though completely erroneous idea, often held by students and laymen, is that theory is synonymous with speculation. The idea seems to be that theory refers to ideas which have never been tested. If theories are ever put to the test and they prove to be right, then the theories disappear and they are replaced by facts, or perhaps even laws. This unfortunate way of thinking that theory is purely speculative leads to a division, not only between the concept of theory and fact, but also between sociological theorists and what are sometimes called sociological empiricists or even simply field workers. The truth of the matter is that theory is derived from findings which are put together, and the logical relations between findings together build up theory. Looked at in this way theory then becomes the ordering of facts and findings in a meaningful way and this ordering and building up is of the very essence of scientific enquiry, since without ordering facts and without putting them into some systematic framework there would be no generalisations and no predictions. But prediction is not synonymous with theory. Theory in fact is the building which is made from the hard won bricks of research studies.

It is sometimes useful to think of the findings of science, that is to say the meaningful observations made and their linking together, as being contributions to a kitty which is the theory of the subject. Looked at in this way one sees empirical observations, facts, research studies, and so on, as contributions to this kitty and the bigger the kitty, the greater the development of the subject itself.

When the findings have been put into the kitty then relationships between facts and relationships between research studies can be seen more clearly and these in turn will lead the knowledgeable sociologist to spotting the points where further enquiry needs to be made. Quite a useful example of this type of work is to be seen in Frankenberg's study of British communities where he begins at one end with studies of the very smallest and most isolated rural communities and moves steadily along to studies carried out in conurbations and very large urban housing estates. Frankenberg points out, from the generalising work which he attempts in his book,[1] that one obvious gap in our knowledge at the present time is the need for a good study to be made of what might be called 'industrialised farming', that is to say a community where agriculture is carried out on a very large scale, with a great deal of managerial and business type expertise being used in what is essentially a rural agricultural setting. Until one has sufficient knowledge of the work carried out in the field and until one attempts, as Frankenberg does, to build up some sort of generalisation in a particular aspect of sociological investigation, one would not be aware of the gaps, and at times in sociology the enormous gaps, which need to be filled by particular studies. So theory is extremely useful in summarising findings, linking them together, putting forward uniformities of social behaviour and then enabling the research worker to move a step further forward with new, relevant studies which themselves will contribute directly to the furtherance of theory. This process of being stimulated by theory to carry out further research, and research contributing to the building up of theory, is essentially what scientists call a 'feed-back mechanism'. The process of scientific research is therefore a continuous one, and seen in this light sociology accumulates its findings and brings them together to build up its generalisations and, if possible, laws of social behaviour. Pointing to gaps in our knowledge, which comes from adequate understanding of sociological theory, is one of the most important parts of sociological research and brings out clearly the importance of the research worker being guided from a good background of theory. This is not to say that some good pieces of research do not emerge from almost accidental findings of research workers. The whole history of science is full of examples of scientists

[1] R. Frankenberg, *Communities in Britain*, Pelican Books, 1966.

happening to notice something almost by accident and being stimulated to ask why this had happened.[2] Why, for example, did apples fall from trees? Why did the kettle lid jump up and down? In recent years, the example of Fleming's discovery of penicillin is a good case of the almost accidental research which was of tremendous value. In social research, perhaps the most quoted case is that of Elton Mayo's[3] study of American girls in a factory, where his observations of the importance of the creation of social groups led to the development of a whole school of thought in social psychology. New facts found by accident may be the starting point for new theories and sociologists are certainly not lacking in opportunities for chance stimulation in their ordinary everyday life since they themselves live amongst the phenomena which they study. The difference of approach illustrated here between the apparently hard working development from carefully formulated theory towards new ideas to be tested where there are gaps in the subject on the one hand and this last mentioned almost accidental following up of ideas that just seem to occur out of the blue, would, on the face of things, seem to make it difficult to bring two such disparate methods of sociological enquiry together into one discipline. But it is by no means difficult if one has a procedure for sociological enquiry and this procedure we shall now consider by working from what is called an empirical approach to enquiry.

Empiricism and Sociology

The Shorter Oxford Dictionary says that empiric means 'based on observation or experiment, not theory'. In general, empiricism is based upon direct experience only and ignores statements based upon anything other than experience. In its extreme form, therefore, empiricism limits itself to the results of direct observation and virtually denies the value of theory since this is generalisation removed from first-hand observation. We are not concerned here with the philosophical aspects of empiricism, but rather we are interested in empiricism as it particularly concerns sociology. The point is an

[2] See W. I. B. Beveridge, *The Art of Scientific Investigation*, London, 1951, for examples.

[3] See especially Elton Mayo, *The Human Problems of an Industrial Civilisation*, Boston, 1946 (2nd edition).

important one, since it is our contention that sociology is more than just a collection of empirical findings, and also more than a set of purely speculative arm-chair theories.

Let us first look at the empirical approach in a concrete instance. Most housewives and many motorists are empiricists. The housewife who knows when her electric iron ceases to work that she must replace the fuse (let us say it is a cartridge fuse in a 13-amp plug) is an empiricist. She observes that by taking out the old fuse and putting a new one in she has caused the iron to work again. Similarly the motorist who discovers that there is a particular amount which he should pull out his choke button so as to get the car to start on a cold morning is also an empiricist. He notes that too little choke does not work, yet too much choke does not help either. Just why the particular setting should be effective does not worry him particularly since he is only concerned with his own car, not motor engineering in general. The practical empiricist is the person who knows where to slap the television set to cure it of flicker, the little dodge that stops the Yorkshire pudding from being flat, the combination of household ingredients (a teaspoonful of salt, a teaspoonful of baking powder in a pint of boiling water in an aluminium container) which clean the tarnish off silver. People who have a 'knack' for things are often empiricists, as are people who do things that granny did because they work. The domestic empiricist is not concerned with the generalities or principles underlying the cooker or the car; he or she sees what has to be done to achieve a desired end and that is that.

At work there is a great deal of empiricism—sometimes it becomes almost a mystique, as in the steel-making process where the head melter is supposed to be able to tell whether the melt is 'done' by spitting into it. A good example of empiricism can be seen in the making of magnets. I once saw a woman whose job it was to make small bar magnets from steel blanks about two inches long. On her right hand she had a large pile of blanks. In front of her she had a large electric coil, suitably insulated, and a button. On her left she had a pile of magnets which she had produced by putting the blanks inside the coil and pressing the button. Since the whole process took only a few seconds for each blank and the woman was working full-time it could not be denied that this woman knew, from her own sensory experience, a great deal about the making of magnets. Probably few people in the country could have more direct experience than she had. But her knowledge of magnet making contained no scraps of theoretical magnetism. She knew nothing about field forces or induction or anything of that sort. She only knew how to make magnets.

Much practical work in agriculture is of an empirical type and the 'practical' farmer is often characterised by his empirical approach as contrasted with perhaps the more theoretically-based approach of his son who has attended agricultural college or university and who understands some of the theory underlying a more scientific approach to agriculture.

Whilst writing the previous chapter I had a personal example of empiricism in medicine. One evening whilst playing tennis I wrenched my right arm very badly and the pain was so bad that the next day I could not use my hand at all. My general practitioner diagnosed a severe case of 'tennis elbow' and sent me to the orthopaedic outpatients clinic of one of the hospitals. There, after X-ray, the doctor gave me an injection of cortisone, which at first increased the pain considerably, but later helped greatly, and after a week my hand was useable again. But the cortisone treatment, as the doctor told me, was quite empirical. The medical profession know *what* the cortisone does, but they cannot explain how it does it. They have no general theory into which this particular action can be placed. If they had then their knowledge of the value of cortisone would be greatly enhanced and they would not be treating 'in the dark'. Obviously one of the dangers of empirical treatment in medicine is that, without general theory, the drug manufacturers may find some drugs which have important, even tragic, side effects. Only when empirical findings can be put together into general theory can better safeguards be provided.

All sciences—physics, agriculture, medicine and even sociology— go beyond the mere solution of immediate problems, whether these problems are of a 'pure' intellectual type, or an 'applied' practical sort. But it is commonplace for studies to begin with fairly practical or unsophisticated problems. From the empirical studies work then goes further and more precise definitions, control of observations, measurement of variables are introduced to add precision to the studies. From these studies, preferably repeated time and time again, we then put results together and seek for links between findings and broader generalisations. In effect, it is as if the woman making the bar magnets suddenly realised that there were more questions to be asked about her job; that pressing the button was not really much of an answer to the question 'How do you make magnets?'. From the generalisations, theory is then built up, tentatively at first, and perhaps very low-level and crude, but always referable back to the original scientific observations and findings.

In this way theory is at once both the broad generalisations which lead the researcher on to further enquiries and the precise statements of inter-relationships which help tidy up some of the loose ends of understanding. In the continuous process thus engendered one sees how true theory stimulates ideas about what may be in realms as yet unexplored. The ideas which come from a good theoretical understanding are termed hypotheses, and this concept is our next one for study.

Hypotheses

We have seen that when facts are assembled together and seen in relationship to each other, generalisations can be made which help to develop theories. The theory is then *not* merely speculation, but is a composition of inter-related facts from which new relationships may be deduced. We do not yet know if these deductions are correct since they are as yet untested. It is in putting forward new ideas, derived from theoretical bases, that the hypothesis has its function. Usually hypotheses seek to refine theory, since the generalisations made may be relatively low-level and crude ones, and the new hypothesis seeks to produce a more sophisticated statement of relationship. Hypotheses, then, help us to refine theory by bringing more details into consideration in areas of research which may previously have only been explored in a rather rough way.

The Webbs defined the hypothesis as 'any tentative supposition, by the aid of which we endeavour to explain facts by discovering their orderliness. . . . Without the guidance of hypotheses we should not know what to observe, what to look for, or what experiment to make in order to discover order in routine.'[4] Since the hypothesis is a tentative supposition, it can normally be stated by beginning with the word 'that'. For example, a hypothesis might be 'that egalitarian-minded academics are working class in their family backgrounds.' This way of putting the hypothesis is useful in that it does two things. Firstly it produced a flat statement of fact which can be put to the test, and, secondly, it states the case in an extreme or 'ideal' form, eschewing such modifications as 'most', or 'a majority'. The second point will be dealt with by the research which is likely to give an answer in percentage form anyway, so no harm is done in stating the hypothesis in the 100 per cent way.[5]

Of course, not all social research, not even all sociological research, is based upon openly stated hypotheses. Much research which contributes useful information to sociology is carried out by non-sociologists, and perhaps the best example of this is the decennial census of population without which British sociology would be hard pressed for much basic data about our society. The population census does not start from sociological theory and does not concern itself with the formulation of explicit hypotheses. It is based on the agreed belief that a regular count of several basic demographic factors is vital for an understanding of the structure of our society, and at each census it is customary to ask certain special questions which deal with current matters of special importance. (In the 1961 census a special 10 per cent sample was given a special questionnaire asking for many more details than were required of the other 90 per cent.) In the past some of the most famous research studies carried out in this country by means of social surveys have not been concerned with testing hypotheses. Neither Charles Booth nor Seebohm Rowntree were sociologists; they were just wealthy men with strong social consciences who were interested in the problems of poverty and were able enough to carry out quite sophisticated studies of this phenomenon in London and York at the end of the nineteenth

[4] S. and B. Webb, op. cit., p. 60.

[5] An interesting hypothesis was reported in *New Society*, 25th August 1966, in an article by Esther R. Goshen-Gottsein in Israel where the hypothesis was 'that the attitudes of women to their first pregnancy are mainly determined by their ethnic origin.'

century. Booth[6] and Rowntree[7] were more concerned with getting a measure of poverty than with trying to devise a general theory about it. The great Merseyside Survey of the 1930's carried out from Liverpool University[1] was primarily concerned with unemployment and poverty, and like its predecessors it sought to provide facts so that social policy could be devised to do something about an agreed social problem. These studies, and the many more of their type which have sought to measure the incidence of certain types of social pathology have contributed enormously to our better understanding of the problems of the twentieth century, but even though Rowntree's concepts of 'primary' and 'secondary' poverty were of tremendous value in discriminating between different sorts of poverty, it cannot be said that any real 'theory' of poverty has developed, although of recent years some interesting attempts have been made to raise the level of discussion on this subject, and Townsend in particular has tried to re-shape the whole concept of poverty.

But in general the feed-back to theory from many social enquiries has been almost incidental, since much research actually concerned with collecting first-hand information has been oriented to solving practical social problems, and much theoretical work has not been backed up by actual field investigations. Such has been the division that in this country to describe a man as a theorist is almost to suggest that he does not engage in field studies. This sad, artificial division between theory and facts is quite unnecessary, but reflects the structure of the sociological profession itself, affected as it is by its history and its own peculiar form of development in this country.

True sociology is never divorced from theory, yet it never builds its theory without facts, and the hypothesis, we contend, is the crucial link between the two. Background knowledge derived from population censuses, market research surveys, government annual abstracts of statistics, historical records and so on, are all grist to the mill of the sociologist. But when scientific method is employed to keep the work of sociology along the lines of a growing discipline

[6] Charles Booth: *Life and Labour of the People of London*, London, 1902–4.

[7] B. Seebohm Rowntree: *Poverty, a Study of Town Life*, London, 1902.

[8] D. Caradog Jones: *The Social Survey of Merseyside*, London, 1934.

then a close relationship between theory, hypothesis and facts must be maintained.

Perhaps this point can best be high-lighted by using examples taken from my own experience over a number of years with under-graduate sociology students at Sheffield who are required to write dissertations for their final degree examinations. In this university we begin on these dissertations early in the second year so that tutors can advise their students in the formulation of the enquiries that are to be made, and so that any prolonged period of field-work can be done in the second long vacation. The hardest task for the tutor is to help the student formulate the problem to be tackled as a *sociological* problem. So often the student comes along with an idea that is social, but not sociological. For instance, students say they are 'interested' in old people, youth clubs, television, local newspapers and so on. There is nothing wrong with being interested in any of these things, but the point is that millions of other people are inter-ested in these things and they are not sociologists. If the dissertation is to be in sociology then it must differ from newspaper reporting or from the writings of a person with a strong social conscience who wishes to right the world's wrongs. The student who comes to his tutor and says from the very beginning that he is interested in a par-ticular sociological theory ('I'm fascinated by Veblen's theory of the leisure class') or an accepted sociological concept ('I would like to work on Weber's concept of charismatic leadership') is very much easier to deal with since the tutor can help him carve out a small area of enquiry in which the theory or concept can be used for the study of a small instance capable of being handled by the student in a limited time and with very limited resources. Some of our best dissertations have come from the better students who had interests in theories or concepts and who saw their relevance to par-ticular situations. One first-class study used concepts of leadership and group dynamics in the study of a local Women's Institute. Another applied Parsonian theory to the structure of a football club (there was some confusion over the problem of goals in this one). Yet another made quite a sophisticated study of a convent school using organisation theory.

In all these successful small scale enquiries the starting point was a sociological one and the students brought sociological thought to bear on a very small instance of some sociological process or structure. The importance of focussing on the manageable instance is well brought out in a quotation from an American text book on statistics. [9] Its author, Margaret Hagood, says: 'Students who are inexperienced in research frequently fail to narrow and focus their efforts to achievable units. When thesis subjects as broad as juvenile delinquency in the South or differential fertility in the U.S.A. are chosen—subjects which transcend any bounds of accomplishment during graduate work and which are not definitely formulated—they are likely to bring the young research person to a state of despair when he realises that the masses of material he has assembled answer no questions, neither confirm nor refute any hypothesis, and yield nothing toward developing a scientific sociology. The beginning social research worker can make most certain the value of his contribution if he narrows his research to very specific problems. By these bits scientific knowledge grows, and by revealing these bits the student learns not only the importance and full meaning of knowledge itself, but also the valid methods of acquiring knowledge. Thus he trains himself eventually to tackle larger problems and to gain insight into the underlying principles by which these limits may be synthesized.'

Whenever I read through these words of wisdom of Hagood's, I think of two things. Firstly, they remind me of the way in which the beginning undergraduate (never mind graduate) is so often introduced to sociology by way of being thrown headlong into the most difficult and abstruse works of sociology as the first work he ever does ('A year on nothing but Durkheim will make a man of him') and secondly they remind me of a girl who came back to university after the second long vacation having started some research (with another tutor who had left that summer, I must note) on 'interpersonal relationships and group structures in an N.U.S. farm camp.' The poor girl had gone off to her camp before she had formulated any hypotheses; she had no idea as to what theory or concepts her work was to throw new light on, and so, to be on the safe side, she had recorded everything she could think of over a period of about

[9] M. Hagood: *Statistics for Sociologists*, New York, 1947.

D

six weeks and her notebooks practically filled a medium sized suitcase. With this rubbish tip of information she then came to me to ask how she could write it up into a dissertation.

Although this was an extreme case, it is by no means unique and practically every university teacher who has supervised an undergraduate dissertation will recognise the problem of trying to write a dissertation backwards. This is to say, taking the data that have already been collected and then trying to find some hypothesis which they can be used to test. It is very difficult to do this satisfactorily, the experienced reader can nearly always see where the joins have been made and, of course, for the student the exercise in beginning research has been carried out the wrong way round. It is all rather like the trial in *Alice in Wonderland*—sentence first, verdict afterwards.

But let us agree that by no means all research stems from reading of published theoretical work or dissatisfaction with the use of concepts. Many ideas in sociology can stem from the idea that just turns up, the hunch or the observation of something that happens in the street which triggers off a line of thought. Since sociology is the study of society it would be a chair-bound discipline indeed if its practitioners did not move about in society looking for ideas. So sociologists can be stimulated by everyday occurrences which they, because of their training, can see with a special sociological perspective and which they can put into a sociological frame of reference. Whatever may be the instigating factor in triggering off a piece of research, whether it is a random observation or a sudden thought in the library, there is a common form of procedure which can be used for the research.

Research Procedure

Although a common form of procedure for research is being recommended here it should not be thought for one moment that a hard and fast programme is being suggested to which every research enquiry must conform. Sociology is happily so varied in its subjects of study that a wide variety of different techniques may be used as a guide for most research projects. For ease of reference the various steps are numbered, but the divisions between the steps should never be thought of as hard and fast.

Step 1: *The Initial Idea*

This is the very first idea which comes to the sociologist suggesting to him a new enquiry. It can happen at any time of day or night and under any circumstances. I, personally, find that the time when I am shaving in the morning is a useful one for ideas just popping up, but for other people (especially female sociologists) other times may be more fruitful. Walking down the street may suggest ideas to the observant person, certainly general reading within and outside sociology itself should suggest ideas about links between certain characteristics. Speculations about social class suggest themselves at many a bus stop. For example, one untested hypothesis which has suggested itself to me many times at a bus stop by the local Children's Hospital is that working class children are permitted to eat an enormous variety of sweets, lollies, potato crisps and so on at practically any time of the day. This does not seem to be so with what appear to be more middle class children. This random observation suggests a beginning point for a study of social class and juvenile eating habits and from then on to class differences in socialisation. But it also suggests, to me, a further enquiry into how one distinguishes in a rough-and-ready way between working class and middle class mothers and their children. In this factors such as dress, speech, behaviour and general appearance would have to be considered systematically.

I have always told my students that a good sociologist is an inveterate eavesdropper, especially in bus queues and buses, and in public places such as cinemas and football matches. This does not condone Peeping Toms who plead that they are merely carrying out unstructured sociological observations, but it does commend to the sociologist keeping his eyes and ears open. The British attitude of reverence to the medical profession is often displayed by the way people talk about their illnesses and treatment of them whilst waiting for buses, and an interesting sociological enquiry into the social status of the medical practitioner, and especially the consultant

('And she was so bad they had to call a specialist in. . . .') could be triggered off from simple observations in everyday life. In many ways the present trend towards personal transport (especially car-travel by sociologists themselves) cuts off the sociologist from useful random seeings and hearings which can stimulate initial hypotheses.

But, charming though the picture may be of a generation of sociologists going around with their eyes popping and their ears flapping, there is more to sociology than just noting what happens in the life of the bus-queue. Sociology is a scientific discipline, and the sociologist should be equally stimulated to new ideas by what he reads. He may well find in discussions with his colleages that a term which is frequently used is being used in all sorts of different ways by different people. I, personally, am very interested in the concept of 'community' and much of my own work in urban sociology can be traced back to a discussion which I recall took place in the staff common room of the Liverpool Social Science department in 1952 when, as a very junior research worker, I realised how little agreement there was on the meaning of this concept amongst the dozen or so people who had been talking for some time about 'community studies'. My own doctoral research was triggered off by this occurrence.

Another starting point for research can be the stimulation which comes from disagreeing with what other people have said or written. To disagree can be very stimulating for one's own ideas, especially if it leads to doing something positive to challenge the ideas with which we are in disagreement. It may be that a book or journal article contains a statement which seems untenable so far as the evidence produced is concerned. It may be that a writer talks about the 'decline' of something (such as church attendance) when he produces no evidence to show that the situation was ever any better in the past anyway. Statements that things have declined (honesty, morality, class consciousness, religious beliefs) are usually claims about phenomena which are difficult to quantify or support by statistics, and general statements of this sort can be useful hypothesis provokers.

Whatever source the intellectual provocation may come from

(and it is a dull student indeed who never finds himself so provoked), sociology does not stop at the initial hypothesis as journalism or television documentaries might do. The sociologist takes a further step.

Step 2: Relating the Initial Idea to Theory

In some cases where the sociologist has been stimulated in his first idea by reading within sociology itself he may find that this step is practically unnecessary. But in the case of the random observation, or the hunch that popped up over a cup of coffee, it may well be a very important and not too easy one.

Let us illustrate this particular step by an example from life. A sociologist was present at the christening in an Anglican church one Sunday when two babies were being baptised. One set of parents were regular church-goers and genuine believers; the other parents had probably never been to church since they were married—they were merely exercising their rights, within the established church, to have their child baptised in the parish church. The initial reaction is to wonder why two sets of parents should be undertaking an identical ritual and yet, obviously, be so different in their approaches to it. The hypothesis is advanced that for one set of parents the baptism is a religious ritual, for the other it is a social one. From this initial thought the sociologist goes on to consider baptism as a 'rite of passage' and he scans the library in both the sociology and the social anthropology sections for previous writings which will tell him more about baptism in other cultures and also about the significance of rites of passage in both primitive and advanced societies. He will undoubtedly find that the very term 'baptism' is a difficult one to use all the time, since it really refers to the rite of immersing in or sprinkling with water as a sign of purification and, with Christian churches, admission to the church. The act of giving the child a name which accompanies the baptism is not explicitly brought out in either the term 'baptism' or the more commonly used 'christening', since the latter, obviously, means making a Christian of the infant. So the sociologist finds himself seeking for concepts amongst descriptions of initiation rites in non-Christian societies and in all this he learns more about the general purposes and beliefs which surround the admission of a young child into the culture into which he has been born. The sociologist then finds that this general picture (the theory) suggests to him certain ideas which may explain why the non-Christian people wish to have their baby undergo a ceremony in a religious belief to which they are not themselves subscribers. And he will find all sorts of possible explanations for the choice of 'God-parents' who are friends of the non-Christian couple, equally non-religious and yet quite happy to vow that they will, in the name of the child, renounce the devil and all his works, the vain pomp and glory of the world, with all covetous desires of the same, and the carnal desires of the flesh so that they will not follow, nor be led by them. Having renounced all those on the infant's behalf the God-parents will then agree that they steadfastly believe in the creed and the commandments. Made seriously these are very grave undertakings, but no one present pretends for one minute that the second set of God-parents are mouthing agreement to things they even understand, never mind believe. The ceremony, as a *religious* ceremony, is a mockery, yet as a *social* ceremony, with the gathering of relatives and friends, the honour of being asked to be God-parents, the tea-party afterwards and the christening presents given (silver objects in particular) the whole thing has a significant place in the lives of the people concerned.

It is the task of the sociologist to understand all this, to find out what has been done already in this field, to see what light the general background of religious and familial studies can shed on this particular social act, and to formulate his original ideas in a more explicitly sociological fashion. If he does this then he has brought a sociological perspective to bear on the first idea and he is ready to go on to the next step which will be one of limiting his ideas to a feasible work scheme.

Step 3: Limiting the Hypothesis

It may well be that by now the sociologist has decided that the ritual of baptism in modern British society is a social rather than a religious ceremony. But a hypothesis as crude and general as this cannot be satisfactorily tested by dealing with something which is manifestly a religious ceremony, yet we believe (that is, we hypothesise) that for many people its significance is more social than religious. To get to grips with this problem we now have to break up our general hypothesis into a number of smaller ones which can be put to the test. We may find that some of the ideas we want to test are very difficult ones; certainly in using this particular example of baptism we are not taking the easiest idea ever put forward.

In the breaking-down process we find a number of ideas suggesting themselves. We suggest that baptism for non-believers enables a family re-union to take place. We suggest that it enables the parents to pay a compliment to close friends by inviting them to be God-parents. We suggest that the choosing of the names for the child enables the parents to pay compliments to other relatives. We suggest that the act of baptising the child is viewed with superstition as much as religious belief; that it is 'better' for the child to be baptised in case anything happens to it. We suggest that the first-born child tends to get a bigger party and more presents than subsequent children. We suggest that working class people make rather more of a 'thing' of the whole business than do middle class people, irrespective of their religious beliefs. And so on ... with all these 'suggestions' we are putting foward minor hypotheses which we would like to test, because added together they will give us answers to our initial broad hypothesis about baptism. It is worth noticing here that we have already begun to formulate the problem in a more practical way, that we are carving out parts of the general problem which can be *observed*.

The next problem, though, comes when we recognise that the work done so far has produced a piece of research which could happily keep a dozen people occupied for the rest of their lives. We have formulated an idealistic piece of research which we could never hope to carry out with our own (almost certainly) limited money, time and personnel. So having broken down our hypothesis into smaller testable parts we have now to decide how far we can hope to get on our present research project. It is almost certain that we shall not be able to mount a nation-wide sample survey with sub-samples taken from the Scottish Highlands down to the West

Country. We shall probably be conducting a local survey in the area where we ourselves live and work. We may decide that our own contribution at this stage would be most usefully limited to a comparison between middle class and working class groups, and so we decide to do a survey in two such localities. We find it difficult to know how to obtain samples of families with recent baptisms, so we enlist the help of some local clergy who are interested, and we find that it seems more simple to restrict ourselves to baptism within the Anglican church, since other baptisms in non-conformist churches and chapels suggest that the parents are of some definite religious following. Eventually we end up with samples of people who have had children baptised at two Anglican churches, one in a middle class area, the other in a working class area, over the past year. We are ready to approach these people to ask them if they will fill in questionnaires or be interviewed to help us with our research.

At this point let us take stock of the limitations we have put on our research. We have decided to study just one area, at one particular time. That is, we have chosen two parishes in our particular town —and we cannot be sure how typical the parishes or the town are of the rest of the country. This problem of representativeness of our study can be overcome by repeats of our study being made in other parts of the country. Perhaps where we live there is a historical tradition of baptisms being great occasions which is not so in, say, Eastbourne or Hammersmith. In their famous study of kinship in Bethnal Green, Young and Wilmott made this very point when they said, in their introduction, 'The people with whom we had the intensive interviews and from whom we quote are not necessarily pre-resentative of the two districts in which they live. The two marriage samples are not only very small, but some of the people in them were more friendly, more frank and more full than others and therefore bulk larger in our account. . . . If we cannot safely generalise even about the two districts we have come to know, still less, of course, can we generalise from East London to the rest of the country'.[10] Unfortunately there has not been a great deal of testing their ideas out in other areas of London or the rest of the country, so we cannot be at all sure whether the findings they claim are

[10] M. Young and P. Willmott: *Family and Kinship in East London*, London, 1957.

appropriate for application to the whole of our society. But, this is not to criticise Young and Willmott, since they did explicitly stipulate the limitations which should be placed on their work. If we accept the internal validity of their study we should not take the findings beyond the limits they set down themselves. So in sociological surveys the limitations can be very severe, yet it would be foolish to try to avoid them. By reducing the scope of the enquiry we make more certain the worth of what we are doing (always assuming, of course, that the study itself is well conducted) and by describing carefully what we do we make it possible for other researchers to duplicate our own study or conduct a similar one with slightly different variables. The possibilities of repetition and development will depend greatly upon how carefully we conduct our own enquiry, and particularly how we go about the next step, which is that of collecting our data.

Step 4: Collection of Data

The collection of data in sociology may vary widely according to the particular form taken by the research. By no means all sociology is dependent upon field surveys, although they are the main feature of some subsequent chapters in this book. Many sociologists carry out studies which use historical information. J. Banks' study *Prosperity and Parenthood*[11] is chiefly concerned with Victorian England, so that no field survey could have been possible. Other studies may use largely statistical information for their data. Moser and Scott's[12] work on British towns and their social characteristics is a rare example of a highly specialised study in urban sociology in which a computer played a large part. In many sociological enquiries historical and statistical sources may be quite invaluable in supplying information to help test hypotheses, and a field survey in which the first hand collection of data is carried out may not be appropriate. But many research studies do necessitate some collection of original data, simply because the answers to the questions

[11] J. A. Banks: *Prosperity and Parenthood*, London, 1954.
[12] C. A. Moser and W. Scott: *British Towns, a Statistical Study of their Social and Economic Differences*, London, 1961.

being asked cannot be got except by the researcher going out and finding out for himself. The method employed may be a postal questionnaire sent out to hundreds, or even thousands, of possible respondents, in which case the 'going out' is being done rather at one step removed, but in this case the data are actually coming from a sample of people, even though no personal contact is made. When interview surveys are carried out, however, the researcher, or his assistants, must actually make contact, on a face-to-face basis, with the people he is studying. Not all field surveys necessitate formal interviewing, especially in community surveys there may just be one field worker living in the community. But all are concerned with observation of one sort or another, and all need to produce findings which are objective, unbiased, consistent and unambiguous. So far as possible, in the collection of all field data the reader should be able to check the validity of reporting and he should not have to trust the reporter too much.

The collection of data and the general observation stage (often referred to in general terms as 'the field work') can be an onerous step for the inexperienced researcher, particularly if the field work is undertaken too soon, before ideas have been clarified or without adequate pilot studies being made to try out questionnaires or interview schedules. In general, as we shall discuss later, data should be collected because they are relevant—not just because they are interesting. If the criterion of relevancy is adhered to the research worker knows *why* he is collecting information because he knows *what* he is going to use if for. This means that a great deal of preparation needs to be made before the field work begins, and the more planning there is done beforehand, the less wasted time there will be in the field work itself, and the easier will be the next stage, which is the analysis of the data collected.

Step 5: Analysis of Data

The methods of data collection which have been used will determine the methods of analysis. A historical study may require documentary and statistical evidence to test out a number of hypotheses. One fascinating piece of information given in E. R. Wickham's historical study of the church in Victorian Sheffield[13] shows the pattern of pew rentals in the parish church (now the Cathedral) and the point is made very forcibly how few seats were available for the non-renting poor. In historical studies the actual quotation from the appropriate Act of Parliament or the speech from Hansard or the letter from the collected correspondence may be the vital piece of information which needs to be placed in its right position to fill in a sort of jigsaw pattern which gives what can only be the one consistent answer.

But in the contemporary study of an institution such as a factory or a college, it may be necessary to analyse hundreds of question-naires or interview schedules, and this will only be done successfully and without trouble if the research worker knew in advance what he was wanting and how he intended to analyse the data before he collected it. The researcher who collects data on everything under the sun, just because it seems so easy at the time to ask a few more questions about this and that, usually rues the day when the analysis of all the answers has to be carried out. Questions which had no real purpose in the first place are unlikely to be easy to analyse at the answer stage since the researcher is seeking for answers to his hypotheses which will show him if they are to be substantiated or not.

So the well-planned research will not present difficulties at the analysis stage, since the purpose of the answers will have been thought of in advance, and all the analysis really does is to fill in the details. These details then lead the research worker on to his next step which is that of drawing the threads together.

Step 6: Statement of Results

At this stage the initially stated hypotheses will be restated against the data which have been collected to test them, and the retention or discarding of the hypotheses will take place. No sociological research is likely to produce absolutely clear-cut answers; if it were to come out with all the results 100 per cent in support of some hypothesis it would rather suggest that the hypothesis was hardly worth bothering

[13] E. R. Wickham: *Church and People in an Industrial City*, London, 1957.

about in the first place. What does require careful handling in presenting results is the statement of generalities which may be made. Many results, specially from field surveys, may be primarily in the form of statistical tables in which percentages largely tell their own stories. But the author (and his readers) will want some written commentary to accompany the figures and here caution must be exercised in not claiming more than the figures warrant. Ninety-nine per cent is a majority, just as 51 per cent is, but the word 'majority' applied to both of them obscures a world of difference. The writer of the research report will want to draw together his results into a short statement of findings, which probably will be verbal rather than numerical at this stage, and where some sub-hypotheses have been substantiated and others negated the problem is not an easy one. Nevertheless a generalisation is always more acceptable to the reader when it can be traced back to the evidence collected. The suspicious research is that in which it is clear that the author has been disappointed not to have certain hypotheses upheld and he is trying his best to talk (or rather write) his way round the evidence.

At this stage also it will become apparent how a better job could have been done in the research if only more attention had been given to certain factors which had not been thought beforehand to have been of very much importance. It is a complacent sociologist indeed who does not look back on his research findings and wish that he had done things better. The statement of results is the step at which these regrets can be aroused, since they can guide subsequent researchers in the field. They will also be closely linked with the final step in the research which is that of relating the findings to established theory.

Step 7: Feedback to Theory

The last step in the research is where the worker makes his personal contribution to the study of sociology. It will probably not be any grandiose offering (indeed it will probably be all the better for not being grandiose) but if the research has been carried out with scrupulous attention to detail and accuracy and the statement of results does not go beyond the limits justified by the data then a useful craftsmanlike job of work will have been accomplished. Most of science is built up on good solid craftsmanship and it is only rarely that the occasional blinding flash of world-shattering importance ever really occurs. It is a symptom of sociology's low status as a discipline that one feels so many researchers still seem to be seeking for the alchemist's stone, or seeking status by attempting to theorise beyond their means. Similes may be dangerous, but it can be suggested that the man who produces a well-made brick makes a better contribution to housing than does the man who builds a large mansion on insecure foundations. (This little homily seems also to have a biblical flavour to it.) Nevertheless a little humility does not ill become the social scientist, and a contribution to theory, no matter how small, which derives from careful enquiry is more worthy of the accolade of 'scholarship' than is the sweeping generalisation based upon nothing more than arm-chair speculation.

Sources of Data

So far in this book we have emphasised the need for sociology to be a scientific discipline. This cause has been championed not because of the prestige which the word 'science' carries with it, but because it is only through the better employment of scientific method that sociology can hope to develop as a true academic discipline, free from the biases introduced by ideologists or the wishes to sway current social policy.

At this stage, then, the general position has been stated as to how the sociological research worker should approach his task. The next steps will be concerned with getting down to the details of research itself, and an emphasis will be placed on problems of field research. The two main sources of sociological data come from the inner world of the library and the outside world of living people. For ease of reference it is simple to call these two main sources 'paper' and 'people'.

'Paper' sources provide the sociologist with a wealth of information, and it is foolishness to spend long hours mounting field surveys to collect information already obtainable from published sources.

Under the heading of 'paper' we shall consider the uses, and some of the dangers and limitations, of documentary sources such as historical records, diaries, biographies and autobiographies. Statistical sources could be included in this category too, but I feel that since they are normally dealt with in statistics textbooks they can safely be omitted from this volume.

When we later turn to look at 'people' as our sources for data we shall consider various forms of observation (such as participant observation) but we shall be primarily concerned with the interview and the questionnaire as techniques for collection of data from this source.

Our next chapter, therefore, is concerned with paper sources.

4

Documentary Sources of Data

Introduction

In anthropological studies of primitive societies the field worker in the past often had no written sources of information which he could call upon at all. The primitive societies were (and a few still are) pre-literate; written information did not exist. Whilst this obviously placed great limitations on the evidence available to the social anthropologist it also spared him the problems of trying to find out what help he could get from documentary sources. As for the medical practitioner before the discovery of antibiotics, what did not exist did not have to be taken into account.

But most sociologists, and now many social anthropologists also, are dealing with complex literate societies in which the accumulation of documents of one sort or another has been going on for centuries. The reader who has access to the British Museum, or the Oxford or Cambridge University libraries, can call upon virtually everything published in this country, since these libraries receive copies of all books published. Newspapers may go back a couple of centuries or more, and each newspaper office at least will have its own library and records. Today the problem is sometimes that there seems to be too much in the literature, not too little. For the sociologist to derive the maximum amount of benefit from published data he needs to bring some order in to his understanding of it, and for this some classification of documentary sources is needed. It is customary in research to distinguish between the sources of the documents by classifying them: two terms used are 'primary' and 'secondary'.

Primary and Secondary Sources

Primary sources provide data gathered at first hand; that is to say they are original sets of data produced by the people who collected them. They are contrasted with secondary sources, which are data got at second-hand; that is to say sets of data not collected at first-hand but culled from other people's original data.

The distinction between the two types is generally not too difficult to make if one knows enough about the sources of the data. In statements of a numerical type, especially, it is always sensible practice to expect the source to be given with each figure. If an author says that a third of the present holders of dukedoms in this country have been divorced we want to know how he found this out. If he compiled this piece of information himself we have the right to know how he did it. Did he write to all the dukes and get a reply from them all? Has he talked to them and recorded their verbal yes or no? Or has he taken this statement from a book or article written by someone else? If so, who was the other writer, and where can we find where he said it, and what reference did *he* give for the statement?

Obviously no one is going to want to trace every little statement back to its original source every time: life would be unbearable if we were to do this. But the whole principle is that it should be *possible* for the reader always to get back from the secondary to the primary source. It is one of the great drawbacks of much 'popular' social writings in newspapers and magazines that statements are made the validity of which cannot be accepted without more evidence. When a writer says that 'cleaning the family car is now the principal occupation of the British male on a Sunday morning' we have the right to ask how he knows this, and if he himself has not carried out a first-hand investigation of Sunday mornings we want to know who has.

One difficulty of primary sources is that our definition tends to suggest that the writer has collected the information himself. But in much published work there is not just one writer. In the case of the census of population one can hardly say that the Registrar-General himself is the writer. He is certainly the administrative head of a large organisation which is responsible for the census, but he does not collect data personally from even one household. But the census data are regarded as primary data because the Registrar-General's department, as a single entity, collects and analyses the information. If we wish to query the validity of the census data we must look at the methods employed in organising the census, the questionnaires used and the questions asked to decide if the information is satisfactory. But even if we find some points not satisfactory we cannot blame the census office for using suspect secondary sources since they have collected the data for themselves at first hand.

Another interesting problem which can arise in the publication of primary data comes from the writing up by one author of field work carried out by his or her assistants. An unusual form of this type occurred when I was myself collecting historical data about a small town during the course of a local social survey. I was pleased to find that there had been a number of pamphlets on the town published in the late nineteenth and early twentieth century by a keen amateur local historian. These seemed to be excellent local background and I was able to use quite a number of facts from the pamphlets, giving the appropriate reference in each case. But as my historical data grew I discovered, from other sources, statements which contradicted the statements of the local historian and in most cases when I had checked carefully I found that he was inaccurate. One would tend to put these down to human errors, annoying and misleading, in most cases; what we might call sloppy work. But in due course I discovered that the local historian had done very little actual first-hand gathering of data himself; he was a wealthy man and had employed a number of impecunious schoolteachers to be his 'research assistants'. Their mercenary interests were probably greater than their antiquarian ones, and their errors were written up by the historian. The interesting point in this case is that the writer himself did not acknowledge the work of his assistants in his papers, so the reader had no knowledge of the writer's separation from his data.

In some modern research studies one finds that a book may be written by a well-known author, with only the one name appearing on the spine and perhaps the title page. Then, perhaps in the preface, the author refers to some research assistants who have been responsible for collecting data for the study. The work itself *is* a primary source, since the data have not been taken from *other* published sources if they are presented in a survey actually supervised by the writer. But in some instances research assistants may have been primarily concerned with digging out tables from published sources and presenting them to the writer to work on; in this case the data

E

are certainly secondary and practically tertiary. With so much team research these days it is inevitable that directors of projects must rely on their assistants to produce satisfactory data. Then some *one* person must write up the results (even multi-author publications are not written by people playing duets on the typewriter). It would be niggling to say that where a writer has had assistants his data cease to be primary, but it would also be foolish to ignore the fact that the more people there are involved in a project, the more opportunities there are for errors to creep in.

Another point which may be considered under the heading of primary and secondary sources is the practice, very popular at the present moment, of giving verbatim statements made by respondents in interviews. The practice certainly dates back to Mayhew's survey of London life[1] which contains innumerable passages of what purport to be the actual words of his subjects. Thus Mayhew, who was of course a journalist and not a sociologist, writes of a coster lad as saying of his life, 'On a Sunday I goes out selling, and all I yarns I keeps. As for going to church, why, I can't afford it,—besides to tell the truth, I don't like it well enough. Plays, too, ain't in my line much; I'd sooner go to a dance—it's more livelier. The "penny gaffs" is rather more in my style; the songs are out and out, and makes our gals laugh. The smuttier the better, I thinks; bless you! the gals likes it as much as we do.' The quotations go on in this vein for pages on end for every conceivable sort of occupation. In contemporary sociology, particularly in studies of working class life, we are given passages which are enclosed in quotation marks. Rarely are we told how these passages, sometimes quite lengthy ones, have been gathered. If we were told that the interviewer used a tape-recorder, or that he was an expert shorthand writer, then we would know how these word-for-word quotations were possible. But if we are not told how it was all done once again we, the readers, have a right to doubt the validity of the evidence.

Contemporary and Retrospective Documents

The distinction made so far between primary and secondary sources

[1] See *Mayhew's London*, edited by P. Quennell, Spring Books, London, n.d., p. 84.

can be made even more useful if we adopt a further division of documents between what John Madge,[2] after Gottschalk, calls 'records' and 'reports'. The distinction is that the record is primarily concerned with a translation taking place *now* (e.g. Hansard, an Act of Parliament, a contract between two people, a company's balance sheet, the annual statistics for a government department), whilst the the report is usually written *after* an event has taken place (e.g. a

	PRIMARY	SECONDARY
CONTEMPORARY	Compiled at the time by the writer *Examples:* Court record. Hansard. Census of population. Newspaper report (?) Contracts. Letters. Tape-recording. Film. 'I am writing it now.'	Transcribed from primary contemporary sources *Examples:* Research report based on assistants' field work. Historical study using actual documents. Statistical research based on census data. Research using other peoples' correspondence. 'He wrote it on the spot.'
RETROSPECTIVE	Compiled after the event by the writer. *Examples:* Personal diary. Autobiography. Report on a visit to a given institution. 'I wrote it afterwards.'	Transcribed by primary retrospective sources. *Examples:* Research using diaries or autobiographies. 'He wrote it afterwards.'

newspaper report, an historical account, a practical work essay). For our purposes the essential distinction is between the time when the documents were written and so we will use the terms 'contemporary' and 'retrospective' to describe those documents.

[2] See John Madge: *The Tools of Social Science*, London, 1953, and L. Gottschalk, C. Kluckhohn and R. C. Angell: *The Use of Personal Documents in History, Anthropology and Sociology*, New York, 1945.

With the two contrasting sets, primary and secondary, and contemporary and retrospective, we can construct a two-by-two diagram to illustrate the classifications produced, and for this four-fold classification we give examples (see table on p. 59).

The table does not consist of water-tight compartments, but should rather be regarded as displaying general categories which may run into each other, rather as two sets of continua than as two polar ideal types. Nevertheless the four categories enable us to identify common features of some of the different types of documents which we shall now consider in detail.

Official Records

These should, on the face of things, be the most reliable sources, so long as we can trust the writer. The verbatim Parliamentary record of what is said in the Lords and the Commons is possibly the most trusted document one could find. Any disagreements between speakers in the two houses and the official record are carefully looked into and such is the integrity of the record that any attempt to alter it, except for errors, would undoubtedly result in a national scandal. A member of parliament may regret deeply what he said in the heat of a debate, but he can never have the record changed on the plea 'I didn't mean to say that'. He can only have it corrected if the official Hansard writers can be shown to have misreported what he said. One would also tend to accept verbatim reports of judicial court proceedings, evidence given before Royal Commissions and special committees of enquiry, so long as one can genuinely believe that the shorthand writers[3] were quite impartial, skilled in their work and that all they took down has been printed without editing. But in these cases it is necessary to know what was really going on at the time. Writing at a time of de-Stalinisation in Russia, when the 22nd Congress of the Communist Party took place, and Stalin's mummy was evicted from the Mausoleum, Isaac Deutscher used the words, 'The official, *heavily edited*[4] and misleading reports of the Congress. . . .' Of course, in Russia history is regularly re-written, so we are not

---

[3] At the time of writing the use of tape recorders in law courts is just about to begin.
[4] My italics, *Observer*, 5th November, 1961.

surprised if one record does not tally with a later edition. By the same token, the validity of the verbatim records of criminal trials in totalitarian states is a matter for some doubt. In espionage trials in Russia the accused always plead guilty and ask for lenience, but one cannot know what has gone on before the trial to produce the statements made. At one time in Eastern Europe the trials of priests were regarded as scandals since many of the accused appeared to be drugged. A mere record of what is said, accurate though it might be, would tell only a small, and rather misleading, part of the full story.

Newspapers

Newspaper reports, where a reporter was present at the scene, might be thought to be valuable, but unfortunately it has been shown only too often how little reliance can be placed on them. It is important to recognize under what pressures newspaper correspondents work. Many of them do not have shorthand and use their own personal notation system. Their reporting of speeches is likely to be inaccurate in many ways, sometimes embarrassingly so. Also a reporter can only extract a tiny part from any total occurrence, and in many cases he extracts what will be eye-catching and provocative. Newspapers love a good disaster, and a wedding where the bridegroom's trousers fell down at the altar would stand a far better chance of being reported on than one that went without a hitch. When man bites dog it is news, but the ordinary human recipient of a canine nip would be surprised to have the national press clustered round him. It should also be remembered that newspapers work very fast—the very latest news is always the most desirable, as is instanced by the occasional 'scoop' of the event which has not yet even happened. Reports are cut by sub-editors to fit available space and the particular 'angle' of the newspaper's political policy is sharpened up. In all, it is little short of a miracle that the subsequent report bears any relation to the actual occurrence at all—and sometimes it does not.

Stanley Baldwin, who was once the target of a harsh newspaper campaign, said of his opponent 'press barons'—'Their methods are direct falsehood, misrepresentation, half-truths, the alteration of the speaker's meaning by putting sentences apart from the context, suppression and editorial criticism of speeches which are not reported in the paper.... What the proprietorship of these papers is aiming at is power, but power with responsibility—the prerogative of the harlot through the ages.' (Incidentally, the above reference is a secondary one, taken from Thomson's *England in the Twentieth Century*[5] in which the actual source of Baldwin's speech is not given.)

Some years ago there was a wonderful letter published in the (then) *Manchester Guardian* from a person who signed himself 'Student of the Press'. He had collected together eight different newspaper reports of a highly publicised wedding between a young woman, Ira von Furstenberg, and her (then) first husband. As the bride was only sixteen and moved in 'international circles' in Italy, the press had a day-out on the wedding and 'Student of the Press' noted how the British press 'had shown its enterprise and sturdy individuality. It refuses to conform to any agreed standard even when simple facts are in question.' The various newspapers reported the bride as being anywhere between thirty and seventy minutes late: someone fell into the Grand Canal, but there were four different versions of who it was: estimates of photographers present in the church ranged from 50 to 250 and guests from 250 to 600. Of course, this particular instance was treated as a Venetian holiday by the press, but more serious matters than society weddings show interesting differences in reporting. *Time and Tide*[6] produced a very interesting example of how political events can be differently reported when in December, 1959, King Baudouin visited the Belgian Congo before it was granted its independence. On the same Tuesday the *Daily Mail* report was as follows:

Humiliation of a King   Leopoldville, December 28th.

For twelve humiliating miles today King Baudouin was jeered and catcalled by thousands of Africans shouting for independence. He sat white-faced and tight-lipped as crowds along the route derisively drowned loyal cries of *Vive le roi* with clamorous waves

[5] David Thomson: *England in the 20th Century*, Pelican Books, 1965.
[6] *Time and Tide*, 2nd January, 1960.

of *Vive l'indépendance*. Not since Egypt spurned and dismissed King Farouk has there been such a pathetic royal cavalcade as today's, bringing King Baudouin from the airport.

To keep down the crowds European employers were asked not to give their workers time off to greet the king. But they took the time off anyway, downing tools in the boatyards on the bank of the River Congo to jeer and chant 'Independence'.

Even in the heart of the European quarter I saw African jean-clad Teddy Boys waving their fists at King Baudouin.

The Times report read like this:

Friendly Reception   Brussels, December 28th.

King Baudouin accompanied by M. De Schrijver, the Minister for the Congo, arrived today in Leopoldville by air.

On the 15-mile drive to the royal residence the procession was followed by a helicopter and accompanied by a police escort. No hostility was shown by the Africans who gathered to watch the royal party pass, and there were shouts of 'Long live the King', and 'Independence'. It was a friendly reception and there were no incidents. At the palace the King shook hands with local authorities' representatives including the African mayors.'

The *Time and Tide* headline to the extracts was 'You pays your penny'. The popular press, of course, is often more concerned with entertaining than informing. I recall once, when I was a young research fellow, that my wife and I offered to help a colleague and his wife with some decorating at their bungalow. They had a hall with six doors in it and we felt so sorry for them having to tackle this job that we offered to spend a Sunday with them having a go at the hall and doors. A while later this young couple were the subject of an article on 'Adventures in Homemaking' in one of the largest circulation women's weekly magazines in this country. My wife and I were intrigued to find that the staff writer for the magazine had this to say:

The quickest way to get your decorating done is to throw a party! That's the way X and Y[7] got their hall done. An all white job

[7] As these two people are still our friends I would not want to wreck that friendship by disclosing their names.

from ceiling to skirting boards gave no trouble in matching up. Friends were warned to arrive in old clothes. The party started in the morning and went on to supper time. Y served the working party with endless cups of coffee, there was a stew for lunch and hot dogs and more coffee at knocking off time. At the end of the day the hall was immaculate and charming with white paint.

This description has just the faintest resemblance to what actually happened, but it is so tarted up in its description that we all howled with laughter on reading it. Of course, no one expects a women's magazine to read like Hansard or an article in the Transactions of the Faraday Society (or even a sociological journal) but this particular example is given to show how the popular press so often embroiders on the facts so as to make them more attractive.

The national press must be watched for sensationalism and political slanting, as well as for the natural hazards of sub-editing. Local newspapers, so often useful to the sociologist engaged in a local survey, must be watched for plain inaccuracy at all times. In my own dealings with local reporters over a number of years I have come to despair of ever being reported without something being misreported. There is an old legend that local reporters must always get names right no matter what else they get wrong: this certainly has not happened in many instances I have known. As for quoting what people say, these local newsmen are adept at getting the point of a case quite wrong. It must be remembered that for many journalists the local paper is only a training ground for better things. The ones who succeed pass on to better (?) newspapers at national level, which seems to suggest that the poor are always with us. An example of reporting which leaves the mind in a state of wonder is the following paragraph from a local evening neswpaper which in September 1966 had a report headed

'*Varsity Intake Tops 5,000*. The concluding two paragraphs read as follows:

Sheffield had 19,243 applications for its places, 4,000 more than last year. Its 1,490 places available, meant a drop of 110 on last year's figure, due to Government expansion.

But the 1,490 represents an increase on previous intakes and with an increase in postgraduate students, boosts student numbers to over 5,000.

The above quotation is exactly as the report was printed, right down to the almost random distribution of commas.

Official Statistics

In this country we tend to trust our official governmental statistics and then to distrust the use made of them by politicians. But then it was a politician who coined the phrase, 'Lies, damned lies and statistics' which rather blew the gaff in the first place. The census of population, the monthly and annual Digests of Statistics and the annual statistical reports of the various ministries and other national bodies (such as the Prison Commissioners) and local authorities produce a great deal of extremely valuable data for the sociologist to work on. We will not here go into great details of the dangers of using statistics but merely point to some precautions which must still be taken even when using statistics which are generally regarded as reliable.

Firstly the research worker must be absolutely sure he knows what the statistics are about. In criminal statistics, for example, the definition of a 'crime' is operationally made in a number of ways. Obviously 'crimes known to the police' are greater than 'people prosecuted' which in turn are greater than 'persons found guilty'. To use criminal statistics wisely necessitates some prior work in getting to know the difference between indictable and non-indictable offences and also some legal history so that one does not suddenly discover an enormous decrease in a crime such as stealing cars when the new offence of 'take and drive away' was introduced. The various motoring offences can baffle the uninitiated as I learned to my horror once when on a jury. Although we were trying a man for being 'drunk in charge' two women in the jury room (after a long exposition from the recorder) were quite determined to find him not guilty of 'dangerous driving'—an offence with which he had never been charged.

A popular essay topic for students is often on the use of divorce statistics. Here in particular one can find an increase in divorce which merely reflects new legislation affecting causes for divorce—for example, the Matrimonial Causes Act of 1937 which introduced desertion, cruelty and incurable insanity as further grounds for divorce, adultery having been the only one previously. The extension of legal aid after the 1939–45 war was bound to affect the numbers of people able to avail themselves of this social service. To ignore, or be ignorant of, these factors is to misuse statistics badly, but it is no criticism of the statistics themselves.

The use of index numbers and special ratios should always be undertaken with care since they may contain hidden dangers if one does not know how they are compiled and, very often, how they are 'corrected' for a variety of reasons. It is facile to employ cost of living indices or indices of neo-natal mortality without knowing how the figures are calculated.

Not all 'official' statistics, of course, are governmental, or even quasi-governmental. We would probably accept the newspaper circulation figures put forward by the Audit Bureau of Circulation, and we would probably be happy to quote the readership figures of the Institute of Practitioners in Advertising annual readership survey. But how the first is calculated is probably unknown to most social scientists, and although the problems encountered in gathering the latter are described in detail at the beginning of each annual publication, probably few sociologists bother to read through the technical details.

TAM ratings may be bandied about when sociologists discuss popular culture, but it probably is only the odd person here and there who knows how these ratings are calculated, and how they produce audience figures which are at variance with those of B.B.C. Audience Research, which calculates audiences differently.

Educational statistics are also prone to mislead. If one uses statistics of children in over-crowded classes it is absolutely fundamental to bear in mind that to be over-crowded a primary school class must exceed forty pupils, yet a secondary school class need only top the thirty mark. This is a charming example of how to use different bases for calculations so as to divert attention from the needs of the youngest pupils. Even in universities (where they perhaps ought to be clever enough to deal with these problems) I have heard an assistant registrar say that it is very difficult to calculate the numbers of students on a university's books at any one time, since to define a 'student' is so difficult. (And this does not attempt to enumerate those students who are there only on local authority financed holidays.)

One example of the problems inherent in the use of official statistics will suffice to end this section. Go to the 1961 Census volume and, in a county volume, turn to tables which use the terms 'rooms' and 'households'. Then turn to the early pages where these terms are carefully defined. Then ask yourself if you are absolutely happy about these statistics. If you do not have some slight doubts I shall be surprised.

Diaries, Memoirs and Autobiographies

There may be a number of reasons for keeping a personal diary. In the case of the 'ordinary' person it may just be pleasant to record what has happened each day so that one can at some time in the future spend a nostalgic hour looking back on times past. Probably very few diaries of this sort are kept these days. In days past, when children did not have the delights of the mass media to occupy their time for them diary keeping was regarded as a 'good thing' for the young, just as collecting things was regarded as keeping hands and minds occupied. But today the diary is regarded much more as an appointments *aide memoire*, and for the 'ordinary' person the keeping of a detailed diary of daily events would probably be regarded as just a little eccentric and perhaps even self-centred. Diaries of normality are rare, diaries of abnormality are more well-known—such as the *Diary of Anne Frank* and the recently published *Scroll of Agony*, the diaries of a Warsaw Jew, Chaim Kaplan,[8] who kept a diary from September 1939 until his death which was probably in 1943, the papers being found hidden in a paraffin tin after the war. But even diaries of terror, such as have been published from the records of survivors or victims of totalitarian regimes, were rarely written simply for the author to look back on in years to come—for European Jews there was rarely much hope of any future. The truly personal diary, intended only for personal perusal, is a rare thing.

[8] *Scroll of Agony: the Warsaw Diaries of Chaim A. Kaplan*, London, 1966.

Much more common is the personal diary intended for public consumption at a later date. The publishing world would be badly hit if politicians did not bring forth their diaries from time to time, showing just how they reacted at the time to world events. And in the years since the end of the 1939–45 war there has been such a spate of generals' diaries that it has at times seemed difficult to understand how these men had time for the job in hand, so busy were they with their diaries.

The divisions between diaries, memoirs and autobiographies are not easy to make since one form of record can shade into the other or even contain parts of each other. For our purposes, the divisions could be that a diary is written at the time of the events, memoirs are a writer's recollections of a particular period (perhaps aided by diaries) in which he was not necessarily the central character, whilst an autobiography is an attempt to give a systematic and chronological record of the author's life with himself at the centre of the story. This arbitrary division helps us to focus attention on the importance in such documents of the contemporary recording of events. Whilst a person engaged in a particular happening can rarely see the whole set of events in clear perspective he can record the minutiae of a situation which might well be lost when the position is looked back on at a later date. Published diaries which record a day-to-day chronology of events may not be the most coherent of records, but they do not suffer from being over-edited, tidied up and altered to fit a hindsight on events.

With politicians and military leaders the keeping of a diary is not only the gathering of data for a future book but can also be a form of self-defence preparation for any post-mortems which might be held in the future. In a sense it is a personal keeping of 'the minutes' of what occurred at conferences or in battles which will remind the writer what happened at a precise time in the course of the events. Very few 'raw' diaries are published these days unless, as in the case of wartime victims of concentration camps, they make the greatest impact by the very nature of their rawness and contemporaneity. The memoirs based on diaries, or the autobiography itself enable the writer to make use of the diaries for the basic pattern of events, but by adding hindsight to the diaries a much fuller and perhaps more plausible or self-justifying record can be written. It is upon these sorts of documents that historians frequently draw, especially for the writing of very modern history (i.e. within the past hundred years or so) and it is commonplace to find the historian referring to 'other views' on a particular matter as expressed by some political opponent in *his* memoirs. Thomson's brief history of twentieth-century England gives a number of examples of this sort of thing. On the issue of pre-1935 appeasement of Mussolini over Abyssinia he quotes from L. S. Amery's 'diary', which is referred to in a footnote as *My Political Life*, Vol. III (1955) and also refers to two other accounts of the same events in Viscount Templewood's *Nine Troubled Years*, part II (1954), and Sir Anthony Eden's *Facing the Dictators* (1962). It is interesting to note in these three references the great gap between the time of the events referred to in the history, 1935, and the books referred to, their dates being 1954, 1955 and 1962. It is obvious that only personal documentation at the time could make it possible for these three politicians to write with accuracy anything from twenty years after the events took place.

One of the difficulties of using politicians' or military leaders' diaries lies in the fact that they are always likely to be personal justifications of their own actions at the time, and of course they give the impression that the whole of history consists of political intrigue or war. For the sociologist who is not exclusively interested in politics or militarism some of these diaries, memoirs and autobiographies have relatively little to contribute. What personal records there may be of more general 'social life' have the limitations that their authors are rarely 'ordinary' people. Recollections of high-born people are far more common than those of the low-born. The series of books by Osbert Sitwell on his life are quite fascinating, but by no stretch of the imagination can the Sitwells be equated with ordinary people— indeed it is their eccentricities which fascinate. The autobiography of Princess Marie-Louise[9] is a wonderful collection of recollections of a woman of eighty (as she was when she wrote her autobiography), but the life of a grand-daughter of Queen Victoria gives a somewhat limited insight into ordinary life as lived by the mass of people. Not that the memoirs of royalty and gentry are to be ignored; if sociologists

[9] Princess Marie Louise: *My Memories of Six Reigns*, London, 1956.

would spare a little more time for the study of the upper classes, a far better survey of all our society would be produced. But since the bulk of our population lives working or pretty humdrum middle class lives, it is a lack of documentation of these that is often noticeable. Perhaps one of the best autobiographies (although written in the third person) is Flora Thompson's *Lark Rise to Candleford* followed by her later (and not, in my opinion, as good) *Still Glides the Stream*. Her record of her rural childhood and young adult life at the turn of the century is a fund of sociological insights and is far more fascinating to read, and incomparably better written, than practically any genuinely sociological work of the time. But Flora Thompson was simply a gentle recorder of her own not very exciting life: the beauty of her book lies in the skill of the writing and her ability to make the everyday event of interest to her reader. She was not writing of slum life so as to shock the reader, or even to indulge in nostalgia so as to entertain the reader. The simplicity of her books stand above any attempts to write down to anyone. Such works are rare indeed, and most twentieth century books of this sort, whether written about rural or urban life, seem to find it difficult to avoid the Scylla and Charybdis of sentimentality or sensationalism (or starkness of revelation). The truly talented author who comes from the backwoods or the slums is rarely a normal representative of his class and it is in his hyper-awareness and, often, revulsion against his background that the lack of unbiased perspective is noticeable. In Thomas and Znaniecki's study of the Polish peasant in Europe and America,[10] use is made of a specially commissioned autobiography written by a young man Wladek Wisznienski at the request of the authors. This life history, which extends to 311 pages, deals mainly with the writer's early life in Poland and his travels before coming to America; in fact he only goes to America seventeen pages from the end, at the age of twenty-seven. But to refer to Wladek as 'a typical representative of the culturally passive mass which constitutes in every civilised society the enormous majority of the population' is to do less than justice to a tale which is at times very lively indeed and which was surely not written by any

[10] W. I. Thomas and F. Znaniecki: *The Polish Peasant in Europe and America*, 2nd edition, N.Y., 1927.

'passive' sort of person. After all, how many educated young people of twenty-seven could produce 300 page life histories, even today?

If we must be so very careful then in using what people write about themselves, would we be any better to turn to what other people have to write? Are biographical works likely to be more reliable?

Biographies

A general glance along the shelves of any decent public library will show how very much the English borrower enjoys reading about other people's lives. Autobiographies and biographies are avidly read and often appear high in the lists of best sellers of the day. In this section we shall concentrate on the biography, since there are special points to be considered about the book written about 'A' by 'B'.

First of all, let us consider the basic difference of approach to autobiography and biography. In the previous section we have seen how public figures often write about themselves for a variety of reasons—one of which could just be straightforward self-centred-ness. But unless a person is willing to subsidise the publication of his own autobiography or memoirs, he must convince a level-headed publisher that the book will pay its way. The autobiography of a nobody must have some sales appeal. In the case of the biography the author is even less likely to be attracted to writing at second-hand about a nobody, and what is more, he has a completely open choice of all the somebodies that he chooses to tackle. The biographer, therefore, is likely to work on people of some fame, whatever may be their spheres of activity, and so the biography is more likely to be about the famous (or notorious) person, the outstanding success or the eye-catching unusual personality. Controversial figures in public life, such as Winston Churchill, Lloyd George, Earl Haig, Lawrence of Arabia, Bernard Shaw, and many others will probably attract biographers for years to come because it is felt that there are still new things to be said about them, new perspectives in which their work can be seen, and new interpretations of politics or the arts in which their contributions should be judged. But even if we tend to look for the scholarly, non-involved biography of the great man or woman we cannot be sure that the work will be beyond criticism. Even scholars form schools of thought, and it would be naïve of the sociologist (especially the academic sociologist) to think that his historian or English colleague was blessedly free from personal bias in his views on people and their parts in the history of politics or the arts.

Whilst the academic biographer may wish to prove a hypothesis (rather than merely to test it) the professional biographer may present even greater problems. It is sad but undoubtedly true that sensationalism can be used to promote sales in this present day. A biographical study was recently published for which the author was quite strongly criticised by some reviewers for a rather muck-raking approach. The advertising of the book was able to capitalise on these reviews to sell it on its controversial approach to its subject. In other cases of course, the biographer may be concerned with the defence of a dead person, and this is particularly true of biographies written by loving sons or daughters. In yet another instance the biographer may have been commissioned by the family of a person who has died to write a biography with their authorisation and co-operation This latter type of biography must be particularly carefully scrutinised since it is hardly likely to contain much criticism of its subject.

My own first research experience using biographical data was when I was studying the history of housing management in this country and, inevitably, I looked into the work and times of the great Victorian housing management pioneer, Octavia Hill. She was a fascinating person, a founder of the National Trust amongst other good works. But from my own researches it became plain to me that she was very much a person of her times, as compared with Beatrice Webb who became so much a critic of her times. Octavia Hill believed, with most other Victorians, that housing should pay its way; to her housing subsidies were unthinkable. When asked by a governmental committee what people were to do who could not afford 5s. a week rent for a room, her answer was, 'I should have thought that when the cost of living rose the wages must necessarily rise, or something more efficient be done. People must emigrate for

instance. I should leave prices to supply and demand.'[11] She also took
the view that it was not necessary to have water and drains all over
the place. 'If you have water on every floor (of tenement buildings)
this is sufficient for working people. It is no hardship to have to carry
a pail of water along a flat surface.'[12] These quotations are not in any
way intended to disparage Octavia Hill and the work she did. But
the standard biography[13] of her does, in my opinion, leave out too
much of the rather conservative views she held and therefore gives
the impression that Octavia Hill was a rather kindlier and gentler
person than she was. The limitations of her views are just as important as her vision if the researcher is to gain a full perspective of her
work and times. Charity at 4 per cent interest was nothing to be
ashamed of in the nineteenth century and it was much more commonplace for unsatisfactory tenants to be evicted than is the case
today. It is necessary to appreciate these facts if social policy is to be
seen in sociological perspective.

Another interesting point in biographical-historical work is the
use made by later writers of their subjects' own diaries and records.
In an interesting review of two books on the 1914–18 war[14] the historian and critic A. J. P. Taylor wrote, 'There is one piece of advice
which can be given to all generals, successful and otherwise: "Do
not keep a diary". Statesmen usually follow this advice; so do most
ordinary mortals, unless they are intent to provide a figure of fun
for posterity. Generals ignore it, to their subsequent discredit.
Though they are not much good on paper—if they were they would
not be generals—they cannot resist the squat little volumes. Down
each evening go the indiscretions, the jealousies, the blunders and
miscalculations. Sooner or later the diaries are published, and another
military reputation is destroyed.' Taylor goes on to say that both
Earl Haig and Sir Henry Wilson offer the same salutary warning
against the publication of diaries. Wilson rose to become Chief of
the Imperial General Staff at the end of the war and he was made a
viscount, but with the publication of a life based on his diaries

[11] Royal Commission on the Housing of the Working Classes (1885), Minutes of
Evidence, p. 305, Q. 9157.
[12] Ibid., Minutes of Evidence, p. 299, Q.9004.
[13] E. Moberly Bell: *Octavia Hill, a Biography*, London, 1946.
[14] *Observer*, 23rd July 1961.

published in 1927 'Wilson's reputation was blasted. . . . From that moment, he appeared as a political intriguer, and an intriguer on his personal account also'. Taylor goes on to say, 'As to Haig, in Lord Beaverbrook's classic phrase: "With the publication of his Private Papers in 1952, he committed suicide twenty-five years after his death." Every writer now uses these diaries almost to the exclusion of more official sources.' Taylor's review article is concerned partly with the use of Haig's diaries by Alan Clark in *The Donkeys* and Taylor claims, 'A reader who goes back to the sources—say to Haig's diaries—and examines how they are used in this book, will discover that Mr. Clark has twisted the sense again and again: suppressed the limiting phrase, added a slant of his own.' Of the other book reviewed, Basil Collier's *Brasshat: a Biography of Field Marshal Sir Henry Wilson*, Taylor complains that although Collier 'used the full text of Wilson's diaries, forty-one (!) volumes of them', nevertheless 'there are no precise references in a book of more than 300 pages.' This little example is by no means out of the way as a case of what happens when people become embroiled in biographical studies of controversial historical figures. Not all critics are so outspoken as A. J. P. Taylor, but the article referred to demonstrates how biographical work requires a great deal of knowledge of sources and general background if it is to be done with any safety. The mere point that Wilson's own diary ran to forty-one volumes (however small a 'volume' may have been) demonstrates the selectivity which must take place when biographers get to work. The personal interpretation can easily be worked in by leaving certain evidence out.

One last example may be given here to demonstrate the dangers of biographers copying each other's errors. In a delightful article on 'The Art of Biography', André Maurois[15] once wrote, 'Where can the facts be found? Partly of course in printed works, but these must be used with infinite caution and constant checking. Too many biographers copy one another. I remember, when I was writing the biography of Georges Sand, I read in all her biographies that her grandmother had married a certain Comte de Horne, an illegitimate son of Louis XV; that the marriage had not been consummated and that the Comte de Horne had been killed in a duel. I looked up the authentic sources; the Comte de Horne turned out *not* to be an illegitimate son of Louis XV; the marriage *had* been consummated and he had died of indigestion. When I was writing an essay on Bernard Shaw, I read in one biography that he had attended a Wesleyan school and had always been at the bottom of his form. Before printing the essay I thought it safer to send it to Shaw. He returned it with this comment: "I have never been to a Wesleyan school nor been at the bottom of my form!" '[16]

Correspondence—Private and Public

Although these types of data are always mentioned as sources for sociological enquiry there is really only one major piece of research which used them, this being Thomas and Znaniecki's study of the Polish Peasant. Their study used letters between Poles in the U.S.A. and at home to attempt to analyse problems of the integration into American culture of people from a practically feudal home culture. In all 754 letters were purchased at between 10 and 20 cents each and the results were analysed in 50 sets under family names. The letters were obtained by advertising in a Polish-American magazine published in the U.S.A.. Thomas and Znaniecki's whole study was very carefully reviewed by Blumer in 1949 and he came out with a number of general criticisms of the research in which the authors used letters, documents of a wide variety and Wladek's autobiography as data to illustrate their theoretical propositions. Our concern in this section is merely to consider what use could be made *today* of correspondence for sociological purposes. The publication of correspondence between famous people has been used for many years for the purposes of scholastic enquiry. From Shaw's correspondence with Mrs. Patrick Campbell there has been some light thrown on his personal life and general outlook. Political correspondence can be a vital source for political history, and an American scholar, Professor Thomas Copeland has been working on the correspondence of Edmund Burke in the Sheffield City Library collection since 1955, and has several years to go yet.

For specifically sociological purposes, however, there are likely to

[16] *Time and Tide*, 19th October, 1957.

be few types of correspondence which come easily to hand, and even if they did, of what value could they be? It is obvious today that 'collections' of correspondence will be of historical value; today there is not the same sort of letter writing as in the past in days when people had no telephones and were not so mobile. It is probably only young lovers today who are separated for some reason or another who keep their sweetheart's letters, and the publication of these would be excruciatingly embarrassing to everyone. Apart from this uncertain source it is hard to think of letters which could be obtained after the correspondence had taken place. The contrast intended here is against correspondence which would take place between people with fore-knowledge that it would be used for research (for example —a study of the problems of families separated because of the husband working away from home). But for people to write 'personal' correspondence knowing that a stranger was to analyse it would be so inhibiting as to destroy the whole sense of the privacy of the letters before they began. And to suggest to the recipient that the researcher would purchase the letters without the writer knowing would be highly unethical and probably personally dangerous. The use of correspondence would therefore seem to be virtually nil unless the letters were historical.

But even if letters are available for research (perhaps a secret cache is discovered in an old house) they still have their limitations. Skill in letter writing is by no means evenly distributed among the population and letter writers cannot be said to be representative of a general population. Also in writing of events the writer is certain to have to abbreviate any descriptions very sharply. To give a full description of even a simple evening out at the theatre could cover numerous pages, and it is unlikely that the writer has the time or wish to do this. So letters condense events enormously, and they are also probably written from a particular angle with the recipient in view. One can imagine a university student writing two letters, one to his parents and the other to his best friend, in which he said what the rag dance last Saturday had been like. It is very unlikely that the details would be the same for the two recipients.

The nearest approximation to correspondence which suggests itself in modern society is the use of the essay written by young people as a source of data. In two studies[17] of young people and their views on work this technique has been used, and with systematic analysis the evidence can be quite fascinating. Jahoda's study particularly showed some extraordinary ideas that young people had of how they would get on at their first day at work, and Veness used an essay on the writer's life as seen from years hence to demonstrate the young people's expectations of their work careers. These essays could, of course, be written with their tongues in their cheeks by young people who decide to 'send up' the serious research workers—but this is an occupational hazard for all psychologists and sociologists. It is probably easier to get an uninhibited and truthful essay from the younger child rather than the older. At a recent 'parents' evening' given at my own nine year old son's school I was fascinated to see that one large folder contained essays written by the class on the subject 'My Father'. Needless to say, the fathers were intrigued to see how they had been portrayed and a number of home truths undoubtedly made their mark that evening. From a quick survey of the essays, my own general appraisal noted how very often the sons commented on their fathers' interest or lack of interest in sport. Hypothesis provokers of this sort could be valuable starting points for research; after all, the father-son relationship warrants serious research since so many studies have noted the important role of 'Mum'.

Historical Documents

In a sense it is almost impossible to separate out a section on documents which can be called 'historical' since all documents are historical. But conventionally historical documents refer particularly to events of the past about which the main (and probably only) source of information is documentary, the participants now being dead. Even this definition is by no means satisfactory, since there is plenty of history of the twentieth century, and plenty of people alive today who have memories running from its beginning. Nevertheless, the historical document deserves a special category of its own

[17] See Gustav Jahoda: 'Adolescent Attitudes to Starting Work', *Occupational Psychology*, Vol. 23, No. 3, July 1949, and Thelma Veness: *School Leavers*, London, 1962.

since it enables us to note the importance of the links between sociology and history as scholarly disciplines. The sociologist is by no means universally beloved of historians, and I even recall a fairly distinguished historian (now, mercifully, retired) who once referred to sociology as 'an obscene word'. This prejudice against sociology often derives from the historian's belief that sociologists are just bad modern historians. On the other hand sociologists frequently find that historians fail to satisfy because of their lack of general theoretical framework within which their histories are placed; in other words they see the historians as chronologers without frames of reference.

It would be sad for both disciples if old antagonisms were to continue and it is a happy sign that the two disciplines are growing together with the individual work of such social historians as Asa Briggs, and the more institutional getting together such as took place in 1966 when a group of urban historians invited several urban sociologists to join them at a conference on 'The Study of Urban History'.

Sociologists are rarely fully trained historians, even though their education may contain a certain amount of economic, social and political history. Unfortunately the teaching given to sociologists is likely to concentrate on general historical processes and the methodology and techniques of historical investigation are not likely to be taught. This is a sad lack, since only in the scrutiny of sources of information can the sociologist learn fully the pitfalls of the use of historical documents. Of course, sociologists do not usually want to get *too* historically involved, since the depth of study in any particular period of time in which they can so easily become involved can lead them away from their own original sociological purposes. But in a way this is all the more reason for the sociologist to know something about sources of historical documents and the care that must be taken in their use.

Much sociological investigation begins with a historical background. The community study begins with the historical development of the settlement, from village to town; the study of the organisational structure of the trade union can only gain a good perspective by tracing the development through from the inauguration of the union—or probably before then. In all work such as this the sociologist, just like the historian, must turn to documents to establish the sequence of events and to try to understand the processes and interactions that took place in time now past. Perhaps the work centres on detailed analysis of the books of the census enumerators as they become available a hundred years after the census takes place; perhaps the researcher becomes immersed in tracing records of land holdings or he may, yet again, work on the minute books of committees long past. In all probability he will use a combination of sources, some local, some national, some public, some private, some primary, and some secondary. The sociologist, like the historian, is trying to re-assemble events in a way that the jigsaw puzzle player works. The correct parts must be placed next to each other and if they are right then they will interlock and a clear picture is gained. But if parts which do not interlock are forced together then the picture looks wrong. Unfortunately this simile (like most similies) oversimplifies the problems to be met; the jigsaw of history can produce a number of different pictures using the same pieces, so the result is not as clear as it might seem. Facts put together with other facts lead to inferences and interpretations, and it is the task for both historians and sociologists to see that their interpretations stand up to close scrutiny.

Thus one prime warning for the sociologist is that *his* historical work should be based on sound sources, and perhaps the best advice that can be given to him here is to consult the historian for advice before he begins. It is by no means uncommon for sociologists to ask statisticians for advice; unfortunately sociologists too often feel that history is a field for which no training beyond G.C.E. 'O' level is required. The sociologist who dives into historical research without seeking advice from the historian will only waste time and effort in seeking out the correct sources and is likely to use the sources badly if he knows little or nothing about the way in which the documents were compiled. Perhaps the best advice that can be given to the sociologist in this particular field of enquiry is simply—'seek advice.'

Content Analysis

Although not strictly limited to documentary material only, it is appropriate in this section to mention the research procedure which has come to be known as 'content analysis'. Berelson defines this method as 'a research technique for the objective, systematic and quantitative description of the manifest content of communications'.[18] In content analysis of books, magazines and newspapers a system of categorisation is devised so as to test hypotheses about the contents of the publication. Thus content analysis may be used to test hypotheses about the treatment of minority groups in magazine articles, or to enquire into propaganda techniques. Communication by way of radio, television and cinema may also be used for content analysis and comparisons may be made, for example, of the content of a well known novel in its printed form as against its subsequent treatment when filmed. The important point about content analysis is that the content of the communication is analysed by means of systematic, pre-determined categories which often yield quantitative results. A simple example would be to hypothesise that a certain newspaper has given more attention to sport and less to politics since the ownership changed two years ago. Rather than leaving this as an 'impression' of the reader, content analysis would test the impression systematically and see if it is really so.

Conclusions

Looking back over this chapter I am struck by the dreadful pitfalls which seem to beset every step which the sociologist might contemplate taking in documentary research. Far from the naïve assumption that 'if it says so in the book (or the paper, or the report) it must be true', we appear to have cast doubt on every type of written document ever produced with hardly an exception. This might seem to be a deliberate attempt to drive the budding researcher away from the use of documents for research; this is not the intention. Documents are our (and other people's) history. They record events past and the present stands in a causal relationship to the past. To ignore documents is to cut off sociology from the whole process of social change, which is one of the fundamental concepts of the discipline itself.

[18] B. Berelson: *Content Analysis in Communication Research*, Glencoe, 1952.

What has been attempted in this chapter is to warn the reader of some of the fairly elementary pitfalls that occur when documents are used for sociological enquiry. To go into complete details of every form of document could easily fill a large book, or even two. Every document has its contribution to make, but like any other form of evidence it can be used for different purposes. If the sociologist is fore-warned of the dangers of the 'paper jungle' he will not be deterred from entering it, but he will be a far better hunter.

5

People as sources of Data

Introduction

Since, as Pope told us, 'the proper study of mankind is man', it would seem sensible in studying man to use actual living men as our sources of data in many cases of investigation. Much of what people do in society can be observed, often very easily, and since people can talk, and often enjoy doing so, the sociologist can add to his observation the use of the interview. To watch and to listen are two main jobs for the investigator of social interaction.

But the sociologist is watching and listening (let us call them together observing) for a purpose, and that purpose is one of scientific enquiry. It is therefore necessary to use some sort of classification to sort out the various ways in which he might approach the problems of observation. One way is to use two factors, rather in the way that we did for documents, and these two factors will be called 'participation' and 'control'. Both of them can be thought of as being exercised in varying degrees, so that observation of people could be carried out with varying degrees of participation and varying degrees of control. The diagram below gives a general idea of the

Minimum	Participation	Maximum
	'Bird-watching'	Participant Oberservation
Control		
	Laboratory Observation	The Interview

Maximum

application of these two factors, and for illustrative convenience a two-by-two box has been constructed with four illustrative forms of observation in the boxes.

By the term 'participation' is meant the degree of actual involvement of the observer in the situation under observation. Thus when minimal participation takes place the observer keeps himself out of the group he is studying as much as possible. In the ideal situation he is hidden completely from the observed, who are not aware of his presence at all. By contrast, when maximum participation is used, the observer is with and amongst the subjects of observation, as in the case of the interview situation where questions are asked and answers given.

By the term 'control' is meant the degree to which the observation is standardised in the interest of scientific accuracy. Thus an observation would be relatively uncontrolled if the observer had no way of manipulating a social situation for the purposes of his enquiry. In the minimal situation of control, therefore, the observer would simply have to take things as they came. He would not be able to manipulate the situation at all. If observation is broken down into seeing and hearing this would mean that the observer watched or listened to (or both, of course) a social scene which was completely natural and unaffected by his presence. When degrees of control are introduced then the situation does become manipulated by the observer. The laboratory experiment is an obvious case of control, since a complete situation is created by and for the observer. In the situation of verbal interaction the observer intrudes his control by means of standardised questions, perhaps standardised pre-set responses and pre-arranged classification of noting answers on a recording schedule.

Taking the two dimensions together and applying them, as above, in a four-fold scheme, produces what I have called the 'bird-watcher' method, the laboratory observation, participant observation and the standardised interview. These are merely convenient labels to attach to forms of observing people which in the actual live situation are unlikely to be found in a 'pure' form. Nevertheless they are useful enough here to employ as starting points for an examination of ways in which real live people can be studied by the sociologist.

'Bird-watching': Uncontrolled Non-participant

This could be described in its most extreme form of minimal partici-pation and minimal control as 'pure observation' in that it forms a polar type of observation. But the term 'pure' rather like the word 'ideal' as used in the concept 'ideal type' can be misleading if people use the word wrongly. If one thinks of something as 'pure' it carries with it connotations of desirability: probably 'extreme' is a better adjective, but this again has a rather value-laden sound. 'Bird-watching' may not be a completely accurate term to use for the observation of human beings (even young ladies of today) but at least it does suggest what we are concerned with—a way of observ-ing in which the observer is hidden from the observed, who act their parts in a natural setting with no manipulation of their activities being forced upon them. The sociological bird-watcher, rather like his ornithological counterpart, hides himself from view, watches what happens and records those actions which are relevant to his study. The ornithologist has the problem of overcoming his differ-ence from the birds, the sociologist is lucky in that he *is* one of the birds himself in many instances, and so his camouflage problem is not so great.

One way in which bird-watching has been used profitably is in the study of the play activities of children. From a well-chosen window, and masked by convenient net curtains, the sociologist can sit and observe the completely natural behaviour of young children in playground, street and garden. The advantage here is obvious— that there is no intervention at all in the social setting. Whatever occurs, no one can say that it was falsely brought about because the group was conscious of being watched. But an obvious drawback is the limitation that the observer works under concerning the total situation. If he is lucky he may be able to hear what is going on as well as just seeing. He may even have a concealed microphone near the group being watched, or perhaps a very good microphone on the window-ledge may pick up voices well enough. What the observer in this situation cannot do is to intervene at all in what is going on. So if two small children in a play group go into a corner of the sand-pit, mutter together and then suddenly attack another child, the bird-watcher can only guess at what is going on. Of course, in some situations he may have previous knowledge of the group members which in itself is significant. Thus he realises that the clump over the ear given by the six-year-old boy to a four-year-old girl is merely a brother indicating to a younger sister that he disagrees mildly with her. Without a knowledge of the kin relationship between the two, the observer might mistake such an action for a show of aggression. The limitations of watching from behind lace curtains are obvious and the frustrations of not being able to know all of what is going on must have been experienced by many thousands of urban housewives unaware that they were employing sociological techniques of observation. But just as the housewife gets *some* idea of what is going on by using this technique, so can the sociologist get *some* idea, often quite invaluable at an early stage of the research. Some academic sociologists use this form of observation too little and spend too much time working out hypotheses and interviewing schedules before they have had a chance to see what goes on in an 'ordinary' situation. Of course it is not always easy to observe unseen without special aids such as peep-holes. The sociologist who wanted to observe the ordinary behaviour of young women in a hall of residence using this technique would probably end up in court. But the technique can be used in many socially approved circumstances and most certainly can be of value at the 'hypothesis seeking' stage of an enquiry. The old adage that the spectator sees most of the game is highly relevant to this method; the observer may not *understand* the game at the very beginning of his observations, but it is surely worthwhile going and observing rather than trying to understand without using the opportunities for observation which so often present themselves. Bird-watching, then, has considerable limitations, but as a preparatory stage of enquiry it has its place.

Laboratory Observation: Controlled non-participant

In this method the actors under observation are placed in an environment which is under the control of the observer, but the observation takes place without the observer taking part in the interaction himself. Whether the actual environment is outdoor or indoor the situation is rather of a laboratory type. In fact this form of observation is more usually employed by psychologists than sociologists, since it tends to focus observation on the individuals rather than the groups, but in the fields of common interest to the two disciplines, such as social psychology and the sociology of small groups, this form of observation has its place.

Examples of work which use this sort of technique include studies such as those carried out by Robert F. Bales in his studies of interaction process analysis at Harvard.[1] Bales' work was pioneering in the application of observation room studies to a sociological rather than psychological theoretical framework. People under study were placed in a meeting room and seen by the experimenters, through one-way mirrors, from the observation room. As well as all the speech being recorded on tape, trained observers classified verbal interaction according to predetermined categories. Instances of agreeing, disagreeing, and so on may be noted and the significant factors in displays of leadership patterns traced.

Another example is one carried out by psychologists in which two people were asked to help in an experiment in a laboratory which required them to fit four pieces of wood together so as to form a hanging square. From the ceiling hung a cord which went through the centre of two pieces of wood. Two other pieces had to be fitted between them, at right angles, to make a square which would balance correctly and still hang from the cord. The pieces of wood were several feet long and it needed two people to do the job since

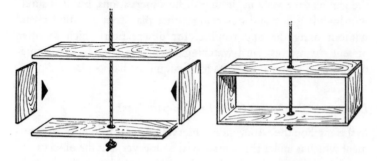

[1] For a useful methodological discussion of Bales' work see J. Madge: *The Origins of Scientific Sociology*, London, 1963, p. 424, *et seq.*

two hands were not enough. The volunteers were told that the experiment was designed as one of manual dexterity and the time taken to do the job would be recorded. But in fact as much attention was given to the way in which the participants co-operated since patterns of leadership and subordination in an unstructured situation were the real focus of the study. What the two people did was observed and what they said to each other was recorded; the action of balancing the pieces of wood was really only of peripheral interest.

A further example of a quasi-laboratory situation is the study in the 1930's pioneered by Lewin, Lippitt and White[2] who compared the effects of autocratic, democratic and *laissez faire* leadership on after-school clubs composed of schoolboys. In the autocratic group the leader directed the activities himself all the time and remained aloof from it. In the democratic group there was discussion of proposed activities and the final decision was always taken by the boys. In the *laissez faire* group the leader did nothing unless asked and never offered help voluntarily. The results were interesting in showing that the democratic group got the most done with the least friction.

These examples, drawn mainly from social-psychological research show how a controlled situation can be used for the purposes of non-participant observation. In the case of Lippitt's study the control was actually exercised by group leaders who were participating in the experiment, but observation of the group was also carried out by other observers. It can be seen that this method of observation raises ethical problems about the rights of using people in these situations. Many people react against television programmes of the 'candid camera' sort. In social situations where the observed are large in number the method rapidly becomes more difficult to employ, whether there are ethical scruples or not. It is not easy to create permanent groupings, such as housing estates, simply for the purposes of non-participant observation. If experimental houses are built and consumer usage is to be studied then the normal method is simply to send interviewers to talk to the occupants. Hidden cameras

[2] For a brief description of this and similar studies J. A. C. Brown: *The Social Psychology of Industry*, Pelican Books, 1954.

and microphones under such circumstances would reek of the James Bond type of espionage.

Participant Observation

The term 'participant observation' is used quite commonly to describe rather different sorts of research methods, and in the very diffuseness of methods used under this umbrella term there lies a danger. Participant observation usually refers to a situation where the observer becomes as near as may be a member of the group he is studying and participates in their normal activities. The term was originally used by Hader and Lindeman[3] to refer to work done in industrial consultation committees where actual members of the committee were trained to observe what happened at meetings in detail and then were questioned afterwards by research workers—rather like an intelligence office might question the crew of an aircraft after a raid. But the term has also been used to refer to the work done by anthropologists who have lived with tribes they have studied.

In his section on this method of enquiry John Madge says that 'when the heart of the observer is made to beat as the heart of any other member of the group under observation, rather than as that of a detached emissary from some distant laboratory, then he has earned the title of participant observer'.[4] Madge's argument for the use of participant observation is that the ordinary interview situation is such a highly artificial social situation that both questioner and informant are in false positions. The interviewer is trying to be objective and scientific yet he has to establish and maintain 'rapport' if he is to get a good interview. The informant is trying to co-operate in this artificial situation yet he is being told to act and talk 'naturally'. Lacking a common purpose in this situation the inferences made by the interviewer could be quite wrong. Far better to make sure that the inferences are correct ones, and this can be done by making sure that the observer and observed are thinking together, not in opposition.

Participant observation, then, is an attempt to put both observer and observed 'on the same side' by making the observer a member

[3] J. J. Hader and E. C. Lindeman: *Dynamic Social Research*, London, 1933.
[4] J. Madge: *The Tools of Social Science*, London, 1953, p. 131

of the group so that he can experience what they experience and work within their frame of reference. Ideally the participant observer is virtually a spy, since to be accepted completely in a particular status within a group the observer should be thought of as actually being nothing else but the holder of that status. It is on this point that participant observation very often in practice does not match up to the ideal form and some consideration of the situation arising should be made.

If the observer wishes to study, shall we say, the social structure of a particular factory group, then to use participant observation fully, in its ideal sense, he should get a job in the factory in that group and become a member of it. To do this without disclosing his true identity as a researcher requires quite a lot of planning so as to give him a suitable history and background which fits in reasonably with his new status in the factory group. Other things, such as having his insurance card at the works, are necessary, otherwise the clerical staff may become suspicious of this new, supposed, workman. All this then enables the participant observer to become wholly a part of the group and to be accepted by it as one of them. But this extreme form, with all the obvious advantages that it has of no problems of dual status, brings with it other problems of an ethical type. If the researcher does not disclose his true identity then he *is* acting as a spy, and if discovered by the workers he is studying there could arise a rather tricky industrial upset. Also for the researcher himself there is the strain of maintaining a false status and background for some period of time.

In my own undergraduate years I undertook some participant observation of this type in a factory in a north eastern town. My purpose was to make a vacation study of the personnel arrangements in the factory as seen from the employees' viewpoint. A friend of my family was a director and he arranged for me to get a job as an unskilled worker in one of the departments of the works. Apart from one clerk in the wages office who was sworn to secrecy, no one else knew my real identity and I turned up, with my insurance cards, on a Monday morning. My 'background' was very closely related to my genuine background so as to make for ease of acting. Before going to university I had been in the Merchant Navy for nearly four years. This study was in my first long vacation, so I simply left out my year at university and said that I had been in the Merchant Navy, had 'packed it in' and had taken this job until I found something better. As the town in which I was working was a port, this was accepted without difficulty, since ex-seamen are commonplace in the district. My knowledge of foreign parts was, of course, quite genuine, and my ability to roll cigarettes with my fingers (unaided by the little machines with rollers) confirmed my ex-seaman status. My job brought me into a group of unskilled and semi-skilled men working on a production line of engineering implements. My work was very simple and not physically demanding, although often boring, so that I had plenty of opportunity for talking to my fellow workers. Being a northerner myself, accent was no great problem. But my year at university had to be put very forcibly aside, and when one young man spoke of his girl friend who was going to spend two years at a teacher training college so as to get as many degrees as possible, I had to keep my mouth closed and not display any unexpected knowledge of how and where degrees were obtained. Apart from nearly losing my job through an argument with the foreman who talked me into going onto the night-shift for a week and then wanted to keep me on it permanently, the whole period of observation, which was of seven weeks, went without any disasters, and I was able to hand in my notice and leave my work-mates with the story that I was going to push on further south. The participant observation which I undertook was a valuable experience for me, although the study I made as an unsophisticated undergraduate was very crude. At the time I had no scruples about taking on a false role; today I doubt if I could do it again. For seven weeks I was an academic spy, and I do not think that my study justified the falsehood which I carried out—and I would not personally feel that any research, whatever level it may be, does justify this sort of trickery.

But participant observation of this sort is fairly rare. One of the most fascinating uses of it was made by an American writer, John Howard Griffin,[5] who had himself injected with a preparation which gave him a coloured pigmentation and then lived in several towns in the U.S.A. for a month as a negro. This study, not strictly

[5] John Howard Griffin: *Black Like Me*, London, 1962.

academic, but far more enlightening than many a more theoretical study, might be justified for the good it could do to help white people better understand what colour discrimination is like at the receiving end. But this argument is based on social policy and not directly on sociology itself.

In a less extreme situation of participant observation William Whyte's[6] study of American gangs in *Street Corner Society* shows how a deep understanding of groups can be gained by genuinely participating in their actions. In this case Whyte himself was admitted to a certain degree of membership of the gang he studied, but it could hardly be said that he was *wholly* accepted, since his status was always that of an observer and therefore an outsider. This status, which is very similar to that of the anthropologist who goes to live with a primitive tribe, is only a partial form of participant observation and it raises questions as to whether the fact of the observer being known as an observer does not vitiate John Madge's claims for the value of this mode of observation. Obviously a lot depends on the observer himself if his real status is known, if he is an easily adaptable person then he could fit into the group quickly and easily and perhaps not affect the group's actions and discussions at all. Nevertheless a true group member has some sort of role to fulfil and the *known* participant observer is in a difficult position. If, for example, my own status as a university student had been known to the group in which I worked, I could well have been expected to know about factory organisation or labour relations in general and thereby (unwillingly) have been placed in a superior position to that accorded me by the work I did in the factory. A known participant observer could have just as inhibiting effect as an interviewer, indeed perhaps even more since the group members might feel that the observer was a management spy. Understanding of sociological research is by no means widespread in industry and most people in works look to 'practical' benefits of research, and these benefits can often be simply dichotomised as being benefits for 'them' or for 'us'. The known participant can only plead his neutrality in most situations of antagonism or conflict, and in taking this position he must often seem to be a traitor to the temporary status he holds. I sometimes feel that there is

[6] William F. Whyte: *Street Corner Society*, University of Chicago Press, 1949.

rather a similarity between the known participant observer and the managing director's son who is 'working his way' through the factory. Both are known to be in false, temporary statuses, both are virtually unsackable and therefore free from the major sanctions, and both are likely to be viewed with some suspicion by the groups into which they are introduced. Also both are likely to come out after a couple of months thinking that they know what it is like to be one of the workers. They can both go home to their comfortable homes in the better suburbs and regale their friends with harrowing stories of what real work is like.

This may be a grossly over-painted picture, but the argument remains; the known participant observer may or may not get 'inside' the group he studies, the unknown one may well do, but perhaps he ought not to.

The Interview: Controlled Participation

In sociological enquiry the term 'interview' is used to describe a wide range of differing things and it is best to begin with a simple definition which picks out the essential points of the word. The *Shorter Oxford Dictionary* defines interview as 'a meeting of persons face to face, especially for the purpose of formal conference on some point'. The interview is essentially a form of human interaction and may range from the most informal 'chat' to the most carefully pre-coded and carefully systematised set of questions and answers laid out on an interview schedule.

All sociologists whose work takes them out of the library and brings them into contact with living beings are certain to use the interview in their work. John Madge[7] makes a useful distinction between various sorts of people who may be the subject for the sociologist's interview. The 'potentate' may have to be interviewed to obtain permission and goodwill to carry out a study in the institution he controls, such as a factory, office, school or youth club. The 'expert' may have to be interviewed because he has special knowledge of a situation which it is vital for the sociologist to have guidance on. In these interview situations, as Madge carefully points out, there

[7] John Madge: *The Tools of Social Science*, p. 145, et seq.

are special circumstances operating and special precautions to be taken by the interviewer.

But our concern in this section is not with potentates or experts, but with 'ordinary' people who have characteristics, opinions and knowledge which can only be obtained by means of interview. At this point we shall not discuss the relative merits of interview as against a self-completed questionnaire; this will be dealt with later. Our concern here is to consider what sorts of techniques may be used when interviewing *is* used. Both interview surveys and questionnaire surveys are aimed at collecting information from people themselves. By interviewing people we can obviously obtain a great deal of information in a relatively short time. What is the main point of the interview?

Perhaps the best way to consider the interview is to consider first what stage the research has reached. If we are at an early stage of the work, still looking around for ideas and still perhaps 'hypothesis seeking' it is likely that we shall want to talk to people to try to get help, stimulation, new view-points and so on. It seems rather grandiose to label the talk with a colleague in the same office or department as 'interview', but in some ways it could be considered to be one, especially if our colleague is an expert of some sort in the field we ourselves have become interested in. But usually we think of the early idea-seeking interview as being with a non-expert, an 'ordinary' person who does not have any particular consultant status. The position can be illustrated simply by thinking of a study that is to take place of the social workings of a youth club to test out some hypothesis about the manifest and latent functions of this association. Obviously we would have to be prepared to see the potentates who control the club to obtain permission to work in it. We would almost certainly have talks with the club leader, the expert, for his knowledge and views. But the 'ordinary' people in this case would be the members of the club itself, and we would probably be thinking of testing our hypotheses by interviewing a sample of the club members.

The main point here then is that the expert (or experts) is interviewed as an individual with special knowledge. The ordinary people are interviewed because they are representatives of the group which we are studying, and as such their characteristics, opinions and so on are only of interest because they can be added together to present the general picture of the group itself. To interview only one club member and say that he could be taken as representative of the whole club membership, perhaps several hundred in number, would be unsupportable. But on the other side, it is not necessary to interview everyone in the club if the proper statistical sampling rules are obeyed and if proper tests of significance are applied to results obtained. The sample survey is a fully recognised method of enquiry in common everyday use by sociologists, economists, psychologists, public-opinion pollsters, market researchers and many other bodies. What sort of interviews will be used will depend largely upon the theoretical orientation of the survey being made. The market research survey to find out what brand of toothpaste housewives prefer is not likely to be based on very much sociological theory. A survey of the mental image of the sausage amongst housewives (this example is not made up) may use psychological *techniques* but is unlikely to be tied up with much basic psychological theory. Consumer surveys rarely (more is the pity) derive from sociological theory, and thus what can be used from them in a factual way may be relevant to sociology but has to be slotted in where it can be most usefully employed.

In our consideration of the interview for *sociological* enquiry we must always remind ourselves that the survey is merely a particular tool for collecting information which is deemed relevant for the testing of a hypothesis which stems from theory. The sociologically based interview has thus rather more to it than merely a test of the reaction to Brand X. Here a difficulty does arise though, and it is best to face up to it right away. Many people carry out interviews and write them up from a social point of view. Newspaper reporters do this all the time and what John Rex called 'Sunday paper sociology' is now an accepted part of the content of the better class newspapers. Books, too, are written with the results of interviews used to give 'human interest'. Often the interviews are very readable material indeed. But these are not sociology. The newspaper reporters, the commercial writers and the popularisers may have great social insight and great interviewing skills, but their work is very likely to be strongly value-laden and biased and they are not working for the development of sociological theory. With this in mind one can see then that for the purposes of *sociological* enquiry the form of the interview must always be ultimately referable to its value in the advancement of sociological theory.

This means that it is not always necessary to think of the interview as only of the highly standardised sample survey type. It may well be that a particular piece of research needs to focus on selected people for information, and the information gained from them will be fitted together into a coherent and consistent pattern with virtually no percentages and significance tests at all. This sort of interviewing could well be characteristic of a community survey where the researcher went from person to person linking up kinship networks, occupational groups, recreational groups, religious bodies and so on. These people would not be experts, but would simply be key participants with useful knowledge, whose interviews would yield far more useful information than a random survey of the community. In particular, if a historical perspective enters into the survey it may well be quite invaluable to interview old people for their memories of the community as it was so many years ago.

If this argument seems to be saying that interviews can be any old thing at all, perhaps this is not too bad an idea. There is sometimes an impression abroad that the interview is only relevant to the standardised situation in a carefully drawn sample survey, and whilst the sample survey *is* an important aspect of sociological enquiry (as the next chapter will explain) there are many other instances outside the sample survey in which the interview is of great value to sociology.

Let us consider then what might be called the continuum of control in the interview situation; the one end of the continuum where there is the minimal amount of control can be called the situation of the 'informal interview' and the other end, where there is maximum control may be called the 'formal interview'. This way of describing the interviews can be used to consider what the control is exercised over, and where the sorts of interviews can most usefully be employed.

Informal Interviews

The most informal interview will be that one where the interviewer, having once started the interview off on the theme in which he is interested allows the informant to dictate the subsequent situation. The interviewer is likely to have a few headings which he uses to stimulate the informant to talk, but beyond this he simply listens. Since an interview is essentially a stimulus-response situation this means that there is very little standardisation of either the stimuli or the recording of the responses. For instance, if the interviewer is carrying out an interview with an old inhabitant of a village to try to find out what the community life was like fifty years ago he will probably have a set of categories for enquiry. Work, leisure, social stratification, social control, patterns of family life, the church and so on will be likely headings used to stimulate the respondent to talking about the past. Obviously these categories could be introduced very simply into the interview and the informant would just tell what memories came back to him. The problem of how to record all he said would be best dealt with by means of a tape recorder so that the complete verbatim record could be kept and referred to when needed later. Otherwise, if the interviewer did not have shorthand, some form of selective recording (probably using a great deal of personal abbreviations) would be needed.

Given these 'administrative' problems of the informal interview, what advantages and disadvantages does it have? One obvious advantage is that, as a social situation, the informal interview is very natural; the conversation flows much more like two people who have a common interest having a talk together. There is not the amount of direct questioning that could give an interview the air of a lawyer and witness relationship. The informant has a great deal more liberty to range as he wishes and to develop his ideas, and this 'freedom to roam' can be extremely useful in getting to the bottom of complex social situations and happenings. Rather than just giving a 'yes' or 'no' to a carefully put question from the interviewer the informant himself can control much more the direction of the discussion and he himself can therefore decide what is or is not relevant to a particular situation. This enables the interviewer to burrow much further into the complexities of some situations and may well introduce him to relevant factors which he had not thought of before at all. When these new factors are brought out by the informant the interviewer can then follow them up in more detail by a simple prompt such as 'Tell me more about what happened when the old vicar died and this new man came who fell out with the schoolmaster.' Given such prompts, many informants may then go on for hours with their recollections and reminiscences.

At its most extreme limits of informality the interview could be carried out with the interviewer taking no notes or tape recording at all. In this form the interview would be as near as possible just like a personal discussion between two people with a common interest. It is sometimes suggested that the absence of note taking can be a help to the informant, in that it frees him from the inhibitory effects of a recorder and a note book. But, on the other hand, the informant who sees the interviewer making no record of what he says is just as likely to wonder why notes are *not* being taken. If what he has to say is worth hearing, why isn't the interviewer recording what he says? There is no evidence that research is at all hampered by note-taking, and many interviews of a very personal kind are now carried out using tape recorders or notebooks.

Undoubtedly then the informal interview can produce fascinating results, and the interviewer can gain real 'depth' and insight into what may be very complex social situations. The disadvantages however stem from the limitations of this form of interview as a scientific tool. In the informal interview it is apparent that a great deal depends on the skill of the interviewer, and perhaps two interviewers might get different responses from the same person in interviews purporting to cover the same topics. People can relatively easily be stimulated to talk about things in a special way. For example, if a person is being asked about his educational background one interviewer could encourage him to talk about the criticisms he could offer of it, whilst another interviewer could concentrate on the benefits he received from it. On matters where there are social inhibitions about declaring one's most personal views or experiences, such as in sexual matters, family relationships, social class, religion and perhaps politics, it is obvious that informal interviewing could develop different approaches to these themes quite easily, and these are some of the central themes with which sociology is concerned.

The situation is then that the informal interview is open to question in a number of ways. If someone else came along and interviewed these people on the same topics would he get the same responses? Has the interviewer used the framework of informality to 'load' the interviews in a particular way? How can we be sure that the topics were put to a number of people in the same way; that is, were they all responding to the same stimuli? How much of what the informants said was discarded by the interviewer because he did not find it useful—and by what criteria did he decide what was useful and what was not? One particularly searching way of appraising informal interviews is to ask ourselves how much we accept what the interviewer tells us simply because it fits in with our own preconceptions or biases. If we find that, on the basis of informal interview, the writer is telling us that all working class men love their employers dearly, or that working class boys at grammar schools have no divided loyalties, do we accept these claims or dismiss them? The problem is obviously one of deciding how to appraise the evidence presented to us, and the difficulty of the informal interview is that it is so hard to appraise. In many cases we are virtually being asked to accept the evidence because the writer is putting it to us in a very skilful persuasive way. But this is special pleading, journalism, ideology or various other things; it is not sociology as a science. As sociological consumers we want the claims of the producers to be examined with the same scepticism that the Consumers' Association would have to the claims of manufacturers for their products. We take nothing on trust.

How then can the informal interview be used in sociology in an acceptable way? Two particular functions seem to suit the informal interview. Firstly it is an invaluable *exploratory* technique. In the early stages of an enquiry the sociologist needs to find out all he can about the situation or group which he intends to study. If he formulates detailed hypotheses and produces elaborate questionnaires or interview schedules without first carrying out informal interviews he may well go off in a completely fruitless direction and have only himself to blame when he ends up with several hundred completed forms none of which have asked the right questions about the right key factors. The sociologist is usually an outsider to the situation he is studying. Straight observation, participant observation and informal interviews can all help him to gain a better insight into his chosen field of enquiry. To neglect these techniques is to neglect the possibilities of a deeper, truer sociological understanding of a situation. To rush in and quantify a situation which one does not understand is wasteful of the time of both researchers and informants. The informal interview cannot generally be used to *test* hypotheses very accurately, but it can be used most fruitfully to clarify them and to elaborate them.

The second role of the informal interview can be in an enquiry where the researcher is engaged in exploratory work, often of an academic type. Here one is dealing with social situations which are relatively unexplored and where sample surveys may be quite inappropriate. One piece of research which I contemplated some years ago, but which I did not carry out because I found it too difficult, was to have been a comparison between church-goers and non-church-goers in an urban area. Obviously one can deduce certain differences from what is known already about church-goers; they tend to be older people, middle class, women predominating and so on. But besides this one realises that they must differ in other ways from the non-church-goers. Do they have different sorts of values and beliefs, do they have different social and cultural interests? The list of possible differences is endless. Now one *could* put all these postulated differences down on paper and taking samples of the two groups go off and interview them with all sorts of yes/no questions. But this, I suggest, would be crude and unfruitful. Had I gone on with this research at the *depth* which I had in view I would have undoubtedly used a far more informal interview and, having chosen possible points of differences, I would have introduced these in the interviews and let the informants develop the themes themselves. Undoubtedly some of my own ideas would have been useless and other ideas would have suggested themselves during the interviews. To convince the reader of my findings in any subsequent report on the study I would have had to show that the points made by my informants did produce a coherent and logical pattern. This is not an easy concept to put over, but the analogy of the case presented in the criminal court may be used to illustrate it. The jurymen are asked to hear the evidence and on the basis of the evidence to decide whether or not they think the prosecution have proved, beyond reasonable doubt, that Mr. X was drunk in charge or whatever the crime may be. In the case of the evidence produced by informal interviews we, the readers, are rather in the position of hearing a case put by only one counsel and not the other. The researcher who 'attacks' a social situation would be the prosecution, the researcher who 'defends' would obviously be the defence counsel. We, as jurymen, must listen to one set of evidence only and be prepared to do our own mental cross examination. Like all analogies, this one can mislead as well as help, but if we do feel that a reasonable case is being presented to us, and that the internal evidence of the research fits together coherently and comes to a result which is 'beyond reasonable doubt' then we may be prepared to accept this piece of research, based though it is on informal interviews.

There are two things which can happen after this. We may find that the writer was completely biased in his views and that he falsified his evidence, in which case he is a sociological perjurer and we should hold him in contempt. Secondly we may find that other research refutes the findings of the first study. In this case we must reconstitute ourselves into a court of appeal and go through all the evidence afresh.

The problems of the informal interview, then, are considerable, and they may make us feel that the formal type of interview is much less beset with difficulties and criticisms of lack of scientific method. To see whether this is really so we will, in the next chapter, consider the problems which arise in the use of the formal interview.

6

The Sample Survey with Formal Interviews

Introduction

The formal interview is used here as a term to designate a type of interview in which there is an appreciable amount of control exercised over both the presentation of the questions (stimuli) and the recording of the answers (responses). In this method of interviewing it is likely that the hypotheses will have been clarified so that specific questions are ready for testing, and an interview schedule is to be used so that the stimulus–response situation of the interview can be standardised for a number of interviewers. The answers received will be analysed in tabular form for statistical presentation and so categories of responses must be considered at a relatively early stage. In all, the questions will be governed much more by problems of standardisation and quantification.

In doing this it is likely that much of the richness of the uncontrolled interview will be lost, but the aims of the formal interview are not richness, rather they are uniformity of question from a team of field workers, and rapid quantification of answers for analysis and testing. The two types of interview are by no means in opposition; they are different tools for different tasks. The human element which is so much a part of the informal approach must be standardised if a team is to operate together. The individual interview situations will cease to be case studies and will become representatives in a sample. It should be noted before going any further that for a sample survey to be of any value at all the sampling procedure must be open to scrutiny and stand up to criticism. We shall, therefore, now consider some of the basic issues involved in sampling for social surveys before considering the interview schedules used in them. Further readings in the vast field of statistics are suggested at the end of the book.

Reasons for Sampling

If we want to collect information about some aspect or aspects of a large group (whether the group is made up of people or things) the obvious thing would appear to be a survey of all of them. But in many real-life situations it is not possible to collect information about every case—or the whole 'population' as we call it. For example, a manufacturer of upholstery fabric may want to know how well his cloth wears, so he gives a certain piece of the cloth a standardised 'rubbing' test to see how many rubs it can stand before wearing through. If the manufacturer did this test on every yard of cloth he made he would be left with only worn out cloth for sale. A wholesale buyer of wool or cotton or vegetables or fruit could not hope to inspect every single item he intends buying; what he usually does is to inspect a sample of goods and to base his decision on this. Conversely, the stall holder in the fruit and vegetable market who puts all his best tomatoes at the front of the pile and then fills the customer's bag with soft squelchy ones from the back is deliberately giving the purchaser a false sample. Practically every day in one way or another we carry out some form of sampling for ourselves in our ordinary daily round.

We may find ourselves disagreeing with other people on the basis of sampling; one man may claim that a shirt he bought from a well-known manufacturer wore out in no time at all, whereas his friend says he always buys this make because they wear so well. Probably the first person got an unfortunate sample. We may generalise from very limited samples; for example we may say, according to the words of Michael Flanders and Donald Swann's lovely song of patriotic prejudice that the Irishman 'sleeps in his boots and lies in his teeth', that the Welshman is 'dishonest, little and dark—more like monkey than man' or that the Scotsman is 'mean, bony, blotchy and covered with hair'. But such generalisations as these, whilst perhaps being true for certain individuals of each country, can reasonably be said to be somewhat prejudiced statements based on inadequate sampling.

Today the importance of *good* sampling becomes more important each month as more and more surveys are carried out on sample bases, from national ten per cent samples for the Census of Population to *ad hoc* large-scale surveys for important government commissions and committees. Sampling saves time, labour and, therefore, money and by reducing the numbers of cases involved it allows for a concentration of effort on high quality information about the smaller number of cases involved. But it must be recognised at the outset that as soon as sampling is done the statements made about the cases involved become *probability* statements. Sampling must mean abandoning certainty for probability, but this is not in any way a great problem if sampling is correctly carried out, since the margins of probable error can be calculated in many instances.

Avoiding Bias by Random Sampling

Bias is a problem in all aspects of sociology and no more an important case of bias problems can be found than in sampling. Most samples are based on the concept of 'random sampling', so it is important to understand what is meant by the word random. Yule and Kendall say that 'the selection of an individual from a population is random when each member of the population has the same chance of being chosen'. This is a useful definition because it stresses the basic point of everyone (or everything) having the same chance. One can see from this that random sampling is not at all the same as what we might call 'personal choosing'. If I were to ask a school teacher to choose for me a sample which he considered to be a fair cross-section of his school so that I could interview them for a survey there would almost certainly be a personal bias in the sample given to me. I might well never find out where it was, but it would certainly contain some boys whom the schoolmaster had chosen because he thought they were bright and co-operative and certain boys would almost certainly have been excluded because of their unco-operativeness or lower intelligence. Selection of this sort raises all sorts of problems of the sample being consciously or unconsciously affected by the selector's personal biases.

A further problem of bias comes when the total group (or 'sample frame') from which the sample is taken is inadequate. A simple example may be used here. Suppose one wants to take a sample of all full-time students of a university. Whatever actual technique we use for taking the sample the key thing is that everyone should be 'on the list' in the first place. If a faculty, or department, or a certain special group of students is missed out then the sample itself has not been drawn from the correct population. This could happen for instance if one were using faculty lists of students as the sample frame and there were certain students in special departments who were not in any faculty. This example is a very simple one since it should not be too difficult to put together a list of all students, since by very definition they will be registered with the university. But suppose that we wanted a sample of a rather more difficult group. It is very difficult to sample young people in the general population, since there is no list of them anywhere. For adults, over the age of twenty-one, the electoral role is the normal sample frame, but even this is far from perfect since it is compiled only once each year and many people fail to fill in the necessary forms whilst others may move their address shortly after registering. For young people under twenty-one the problem is tremendous, since to compile a list of such people would require a complete canvas of an area simply asking at every house for details of the under twenty-ones. In Schofield's study *The Sexual Behaviour of Young People* he was primarily interested in those between fifteen and nineteen years of age and faced this very problem. In one area he was fortunate enough to gain access to doctors' lists, which contain the names of most of the population since nearly everyone of every age is registered with a general practitioner. But this list was denied him in subsequent areas and he then used school lists, projecting forward for the people who had left school; but this had many errors and losses with people moving homes. In another area he did actually have a market research firm's field workers going round all the houses asking for young men and women in the age group, and whilst this appeared to give a reasonably accurate sample frame it cost approximately 30s. for every young person found before Schofield's own survey began.

This point leads on to a further problem in sampling, which is non-response. Sampling from out-of-date lists results in large numbers of people who cannot be found. Questionnaires sent by post are not returned and interviews are refused. All these factors reduce the response rate, no matter how good the original sample may have been, so that what may have originally been a reasonable one-in-five sample to begin with ends up as nearer one-in-ten obtained because of losses. Here the great problem is to try to decide if the non-respondents differ in any way from the respondents, and of course in most cases they obviously do in not being interested in the subject of the survey itself.

In all these ways then, sampling has its problems and bias must be guarded against at every step. Some ways of sampling may now be considered.

Steps in Sampling

Let us begin by considering how we might obtain a random sample; that is, one in which each member of the population has the same chance of being chosen. Probably we have in our mind's eye something in the nature of a raffle as being a form of random sampling, and we are right in thinking of this as one method. The raffle or lottery is a form of random sample—in its simplest form the identical little numbered tickets shaken up in a hat and drawn out one by one by the person with his eyes closed. In the case of the 'draw' for the Football Association cup numbered balls are drawn from a bag and each number indicates a club. At a more sophisticated level the premium bond machine 'ERNIE' (electronic random number indicator equipment) is a raffle on a large scale. The ERNIE machine is a mechanised form of sampling by 'random numbers' which has been done for many years in research. In this method the total units are given numbers from 1 onwards and the sample is taken by means of tables of random numbers which can be bought. For instance, suppose we want to take a random sample of ten students from a class of fifty. We could, like a lottery, put each name on a piece of card, all cards being identical, put them into a hat, shake well and take out ten cards. By using random number we could do the job almost the other way round, by using a list of numbers already randomised for us. This way we would give each student on our list a two digit number, from 01 to 50, and then run through a page of random numbers, using them in two digit sets, until we had got ten within the range of 01 to 50. In the table below we would, working downwards, get the numbers 29, 41, 23, 5, 27, 7, 25, 35, 3, 8, 10, 2, 11, 31, 13, 26, and 11 again.

2952	9792	7979	7002	8126
4167	2762	7203	5911	6111
2370	6107	3563	5356	3170
0560	9025	6008	1089	1300

The above twenty sets of four digits are taken from L. H. C. Tippett's 'Random Sampling Numbers' which gives a further 10,380 sets.

It can be seen that a long list of students (or any other units) could be used for a random sample by this means simply by numbering from beginning to end, and this could be done with an automatic increasing numbering stamp. The rule is simply that one uses as many digits as are in the final number (three digits if in hundreds, four if in thousands and so on) and then use the random numbers in appropriate sets. Since books of random numbers contain hundreds of sets of figures and one can work up, down or across, since all is random, there is no problem of running short of numbers.

It may seem that these two methods are too time-consuming when one could just as well take every nth name from the list for one's sample. In the case of the ten out of fifty students why not just think of a number from one to ten and then take every tenth name from there on? This is what Moser calls 'quasi-random' sampling in that it is almost but not quite random. The main reason why it is not completely random is that one cannot be sure in every list that the nth name does not have some significance. It could be, for instance, that every tenth house in a street coincides with a building plan which has larger houses at intervals and these are over-sampled. It might be that in a list of names every tenth name is the leader of a section of ten people; to sample by every tenth would then result in either a sample of nothing but leaders or a sample with no leaders at all. The point is that regular-interval sampling makes every case dependent upon the first choice and so each individual unit does not have the same chance of being sampled. It may also be noted that if this method is employed then the *first* number chosen should be done by random means rather than just 'saying a number between 1 and 10' since it is well known that choices between these limits do not come out anything like randomly—the number 7 being particularly popular.

So far we have considered three ways of sampling directly from a given population, but it may be thought that this direct method has dangers in it. After all, if we want a representative sample of university students we may already know how they are distributed between departments or faculties and random methods, being based on chance, might now and then produce samples heavily biased towards one faculty. Our supposed sample of *university* students might, just by chance, turn out to be nearly all from the faculty of law which may be only a very small faculty. To safeguard against this sort of distortion, yet not interfering basically with our random system, we can build in a sort of screening device which is called stratification.

Stratification

In many populations we are already aware that the units fall into sub-groups of which we would wish to take account in any sampling. For example, in our group of students we would certainly know what sex they were, and we may feel that our sample of 1 in 5 should reflect this fact. Put in the very simplest way then, suppose the group was 30 males and 20 females, our stratified sample would be 6 males and 4 females. We would take 6 men at random from the 30 men, and 4 women at random from the 20 women. Stratification safeguards the representativeness of the sample by ensuring that the known groups in the population are represented fairly in the sample. This is not a departure from random methods, since they are used within the strata, it is simply a job done beforehand as a precaution against freak random results *if* the distribution of the special factors in the population is accurately known beforehand. It can be seen that comparisons between the sub-groups are made much easier if they have been sampled in this way; there is no problem of having to cope with a preponderance of one group and a dearth of another if stratification has taken place beforehand.

Multi-Stage Sampling

This is a further way of sampling using a certain amount of ordering of the units before sampling takes place. Multi-stage sampling can be used when the population is made up of a number of sub-units. Perhaps a military rather than an educational example is the simplest here. One may think of an army brigade as being composed of regiments, regiments made up of battalions, battalions made up of companies and companies made up of platoons. If one wanted to take a sample of soldiers in a particular brigade simple random sampling could mean finding a large number of individual soldiers all over the place in their various units. Multi-stage sampling helps to concentrate the work on a limited number of groups by sampling *groups* first before the individuals are reached. Thus one could take a random sample of the regiments first and then a sample of battalions within those regiments sampled. Next the battalions would be sampled and so on through the companies and platoons until the actual individual soldiers were sampled only from a limited number of platoons instead of from the whole brigade. It is important to note that a pre-supposition of this sort of sampling is that each stage is composed of similar sub-units so that sampling at each stage will not result in unrepresentative samples. This pre-supposes a homogeneity of units which cannot always be supported in fact, but the individual investigator must take decisions on this problem in each case as it arises.

Cluster Sampling

A further way of reducing the spread of sampling is to use what is called cluster sampling, a device by which sub-units are grouped together and work concentrated on them. A simple example in the case of the university student population would be to take the faculties of the university (let us say there are ten just for an example) and take a sample of two of them. These two faculties, randomly chosen, would then be used for the sample with perhaps all the students, or a high proportion of them, being the sample. One can see at once the problem here is whether the faculties of, say, medicine and engineering are a good cross section of the university. For some purposes they might be, for others (particularly in their general lack of women students) they could be quite misleading. But cluster sampling does have value when distances may be real obstacles to conducting enquiries. So a survey of an area, such as a city, might raise genuine problems of getting about to see people, and cluster sampling might sample a number of polling districts and concentrate the interviews in them to the complete exclusion of all the other polling districts. The great danger of cluster sampling is that one must be able to take the clusters together as a total unit if they are to be used for anything more than just cluster comparisons. It is very difficult at times to say whether the clusters do really add up to being representative of the whole. One can see that cluster sampling of a city's schools might result in a complete set of working class schools with no middle class ones at all; or even completely middle with no working. If there *is* prior knowledge of such problems selection along stratification lines is probably preferable.

Quota Sampling

A great deal of heat has been generated in recent years over the problems involved in using what are called 'quota samples' in public opinion research, especially at election times. We cannot here go into all the arguments involved, but the reader should know at least some of the basic facts of quotas. As can be imagined, to obtain reasonable samples of the *general* population for relatively short interviews on such topics as voting behaviour or food preferences can result in a lot of interviewers having to call at a lot of houses all over the towns and cities in the country. How much simpler to station an interviewer at a busy part of the town and have her interview people who are passing by. But obviously we know that interviewers given simply the task of producing say twenty interviews might choose all women of a fairly young age group and we know this is not representative of the population. So we can actually lay down certain guide lines, rather like stratified samples, telling the interviewers that so many interviews should be with men and so many with women, so many in certain age groups and perhaps so many in certain pre-determined socio-economic groups. Since the sex, age and social class distributions for the general population are known it is not difficult to parcel out the interviewers' tasks according to these criteria. So each interviewer goes out hunting for informants who fit into the right boxes—or quotas. These quota controls, as they are called, can be independent or inter-related. In the former case the interviewer may have to get 10 men and 10 women, and these 20 must be composed of 6 under 30, 7 between 30 and 55 and 7 over 55. But sex and age controls do not operate *together* on any one interview. So long as the twenty completed interviews fit these two controls all is well. But if the controls are inter-related then the twenty cases will be divided into 10 men and 10 women and for each sex the age groups will be specified. In this way the interviewer knows she must include, say, three women over 55. If a further control such as social class is added then inter-related controls can make the specifications very limited—the interviewer having to find two women aged 30 to 55, of lower middle class towards the quota of twenty. Obviously independent controls make life easier for interviewers, inter-related controls make for more definitely representative samples. Quota sampling has the attraction of being easier, quicker and cheaper than actual house-to-house calls but there are distinct limitations which reduce its value. One snag is that some statistical tests, especially calculations of sample error, cannot be made on quota sampling because they are not based on *random* sampling. Further problems are particularly the human ones which result in interviewers 'bending' information so as to fill quotas. One can see the temptation of putting a woman down as under 35 if that is just what you need at the end of a hard day when the silly woman turns out in fact to be 38. A further problem of the street quota system is that people on the busiest streets are not always a good sample of the general population. Bus drivers and conductors resting between journeys are an obvious target for quota samples and are commonly over-represented as an occupation in such samples.

Panels

Rather than having to go out to people and ask them to be interviewed or complete questionnaires, it may seem very attractive to
have them safely tied up on a panel where they can be used when
needed. Where information, particularly of a detailed nature, is to
be collected over a period of time the panel has clear attractions.
Both market research and the government social survey use consumer panels of housewives for budget enquiries, finding out what
the housewife spends on what over a given period by means of a
diary of spending. Usually panel members of this sort are paid a
certain sum of money for their trouble, but not enough to affect
their standard of living and relevant purchases. The panel system is
also used by audience research for their reactions to programmes.
The B.B.C. audience resarch department assesses the *numbers* of
people who have listened or viewed programmes each day by means
of daily surveys carried out in the street, but for actual opinions on
programmes it recruits people to listening and viewing panels in the
various regions. The applicants for the panels are selected or rejected
according to the need for representation by age, sex and social class
in accordance with known proportions in the appropriate populations and then the panel members receive questionnaires about
certain programmes and fill in the appropriate slips for those programmes which they happen to listen to or watch. What is called
'duty listening' (or viewing) is discouraged since people are not
supposed to listen or view just because a programme comes up on
the week's list. Here one of the problems of panels becomes clear.
With all the best intentions panel members may be considered to be
specially interested in volunteering for, or accepting an invitation
to join, a certain panel, and after a time the panel member can
become rather too self-conscious and sophisticated. So it is necessary
to change panel membership to stop conditioning from becoming
too strong and this interferes with continuity. Nevertheless, with all
their drawbacks, panels are interesting ways of collecting information and it is rather surprising that they have not been used more in
academic research where ideas rather than pin-point accuracy of
measurement may be the desired goal.

In General about Sampling

What has been said in these few lines about sampling can only hope to be the very lightest of scratches on the surface of what is a vast subject in itself. All that is intended here is that the would-be surveyor and sampler has some indication of the possibilities open in sampling methods and also a warning of the problems which sampling entails. There are numbers of good books on sampling, some of them now particularly aimed at the social scientist, but even the best of books can only deal with problems in fairly general terms. Every survey which involves sampling has its own problems and the sociologist who can call on a statistician for advice should never fail to do so. There is nothing which can be guaranteed to alienate the affections of a statistician more than the sociologist who goes for advice after he has made a mess of the sampling all by himself and needs someone to get him out of his mess.

The Interview Schedule

If the sampling procedure is all right, the representative people from the sample will each be given standardised stimuli (questions) and their responses (answers) will be recorded in a pre-arranged manner. This means that the interview schedule itself has the function of a standardising instrument. If the responses are to be analysed without a great deal of trouble it is probable that the likely answers have been thought of beforehand and that certain likely response categories are already incorporated in the schedule itself. Since the many responses will be presented in a statistical way (that is in tabular form) the well designed schedule will be drafted with an eye to the presentation of the results in a clear and simple fashion. Very often one sees schedules which have never been taken beyond the question-asking stage and one wonders what terrible time and effort must be expended on forcing all sorts of answers into categories later on, especially when mechanical means of analysis, such as punched-cards, are to be used.

The interview schedule, then, is essentially an intermediate stage in research, and it fulfils a variety of functions. It enables a *team* of interviewers to give the same stimuli to informants in the same predetermined order, and to record their responses in a standardised way. This also means that the interviewers are relieved of the problem of having to remember what questions are to be asked, and, even more, the interviewer is relieved of having to enter the responses after the interview has ended, as in the case when no notes are taken, or only sketchy abbreviations of replies are noted during the interview. The well drafted schedule only requires checking afterwards, it does not require another couple of hours' work trying to remember what people said or what one's own peculiar hieroglyphics made during the interview were meant to convey. In many cases the most probable answers can be set down in advance and this helps enormously towards analysis. One good way of judging a well-planned interview schedule of the formal type is to ask 'Could this schedule be handed over to someone else for analysis without them having to go back to the interviewer to ask what certain answers mean?' If the answer is 'no' then there must be ambiguities or inaccuracies in the recording of responses. In large scale national surveys, as carried out regularly by market research firms and the governments' own Social Survey Division of the Central Office of Information interviews may be carried out over the whole country from John o' Groats to Lands End and the people (probably in London) who have the task of making the analysis of several hundred or thousand schedules cannot possibly be for ever phoning through to the interviewers to ask just what some cryptic little scribble opposite question number 15 is supposed to mean.

Of course, not all the information listed in interview schedules will be completely pre-determined answer categories. In some cases what are called open-ended questions will be asked and a verbatim reply may be recorded (if possible). But in many cases of recording factual information, opinions, attitudes and even physical characteristics, such as domestic facilities within a house, work done before the questions are asked, or the observations are made, can be repaid a dozen times over by the ease with which subsequent analysis is carried out.

It is obvious that good interview schedules are important tools for the sociological field worker. Many scientists spend weeks, or even months, in the construction of their own particular research apparatus.

If the sociologist regards the interview schedule (and, as we shall discuss later, the questionnaire) in this way then he will not rush blithely into the field with a schedule which is the product of just a few hours odd jottings on rough paper.

The Design of Schedules

In a book which is actually about statistics, A. L. Bowley[1] once wrote down four rules to guide designers of schedules. They are given below as a starting point for our discussions. Bowley suggested that one should:

(a) Ask for the minimum of information required.
(b) Make sure that questions *can* be answered.
(c) Make sure that questions *will* be answered truthfully.
(d) Make sure that questions *will* be answered and not refused.

Point (a) made by Bowley is a more general and fundamental one than the other three and deserves special comment; it might be called the principle of parsimony. In many cases information can be gained from sources other than interviews. For example, in a closed institution, such as a factory, a school or a prison, the records will give a great deal of information about people who may be included in a survey. Why waste everyone's time asking questions which need not be asked when the information is there already? But also the principle of parsimony should be used to keep the research down to essentials. There are always any number of questions which could be asked in a survey because they seem 'interesting'; but interest is not enough. A question, to be included, should be relevant to the problem being studied. If it is not relevant then it does not matter how 'interesting' it may be. This means that the schedule designer must always be asking himself why questions are being included in his schedule. If he can only argue to himself that they seem 'interesting' it is highly likely that he does not really know why he is putting them in, or what he will do with the answers when he gets them. Like Mr. Micawber he is hoping that 'something will turn up', and this is not the best way to run social surveys.

[1] A. L. Bowley: *Elements of Statistics* (6th Edition), London, 1946.

Bowley's other three points can be taken together since they cover various facets of the same main point—the questions themselves. To ask questions the answers to which people cannot give is a waste of time to everyone—but one does, from time to time, come across schedules which include questions which require such feats of memory or such difficult calculations that no reasonable person can be expected to give an answer. To ask an ordinary person how many times he has visited the cinema during the past year is probably impossible for all except a small number who can quickly say 'never' or else 'regularly once a week without fail'. For other people it is probably impossible. To receive truthful answers from respondents is an expectation upon which all interviews are based. But truthfulness cannot be assumed without fear in every instance. Many aspects of our lives are bound by taboos and by strong feelings. People who are heavy drinkers will probably tend to give answers on the low side when asked about how much they drink, and heavy smokers may well do the same. Yet if asked how many books we have bought over a period we would probably tend to over-estimate. The very fact of suggesting things to people tends to result in inaccuracies. One market research survey into the purchase of a particular brand of pre-prepared pudding named the article and asked housewives how often they bought it. The results totalled four times the actual sales over the period. In other cases we must be careful that questions will not result in refusals to answer. If this does happen the interviewer will have a rather embarrassing situation to overcome before going further. Actual refusals to questions are always, in practice, less than might be expected. Surveys have been carried out on such highly personal subjects as sexual behaviour and venereal diseases quite successfully. Of course, some people will refuse to co-operate at all, but once an interview is under way most people will be prepared to answer questions so long as they seem genuine and relevant. But, for instance, a survey on, let us say, political questions which suddenly came up with questions about husband-wife relations would almost certainly result in the questions being queried at the very least. It could be that the survey was aimed at testing a hypothesis that happily married couples tend to vote more conservatively, whilst unhappily married couples voted more radically, but if this was not apparent to the informant the questions on marital relations would probably seem irrelevant and impertinent. In all, then, the interview schedule must aim to ask a minimum of questions which can and will be answered. To do this it is probably best to work towards the final schedule in a systematic way.

Firstly, the basic hypotheses to be tested must be quite clear and these will immediately suggest the *topics* to be covered. These need not be anything more than the rough headings under which the detailed questions will fall. Once the topics are agreed, questions will be asked which will fill in the finer points of the hypotheses. It is almost certain that classificatory data on informants (e.g. sex, age, marital status, social class) will be relevant to subsequent analyses. The questions can be listed in rough under the headings (some people put each question on a card to begin with) and then they can be moved about so as to produce what seems to be a good 'flow' for the interview.

When this first draft has been done the researcher has something which can be worked on for potential results. If he knows *why* he is asking questions he will be able to see *how* he would produce the the answers to the questions from the survey replies. Dummy blank tables can thus be drawn up before a single interview has even been carried out. The criterion of relevance is here quite crucial. Given that this work has been done, the draft schedule can then be examined in the closest detail and probably torn to shreds.

Points of Detail on the Schedule

Questions come from the object of the research, so there is no real point in framing questions before the areas of enquiry (the topics) have been drawn out. Once the topics are elucidated the data required to test hypotheses will give the questions which need to be asked.

But the data come from the respondents, so they must be considered very carefully before questions are framed. Will they answer? Can they answer? Will they understand the point of this question? It is a very common feature in the first questions drafted by students in schedule designing to ask questions which patently have not been thought about from the respondents' points of view. This means that the schedule designer must for ever be putting himself into the respondents' shoes and trying to imagine what it would be like to be asked this question by a stranger who just turned up a few minutes ago out of the blue. It is natural for a person who has been working towards a survey for several months to overlook the fact that the respondent has never heard of this wonderful enquiry and may be utterly baffled by it; but in this lies a great danger of asking poor questions, insufficiently considered from the respondents' viewpoint.

Many examples can be given of the pitfalls of question designing. One may use the term 'marital status' for analysis purposes, but to ask a woman, 'What is your marital status?' might result in some peculiar answers. Precision is often needed if respondents are not to be confused; to ask a person about his 'family' could mean to a single man his parents and siblings, but to a married man his wife and children. In a survey of student activities one almost insuperable problem was to try to find out how many hours a week various sorts of students spent on 'practical work'. This term meant so many different things to different people that the results were almost impossible to classify. Technical words and jargon words are always potential dangers, but ambiguities in questions are probably even more dangerous. There is a story of a market research interviewer who was questioning a person about ready-sliced cheese. The informant was asked when she last ate a cheese slice and then the question was put 'And what did you have it on?' and back came the answer, 'The settee'.

We will discuss in Chapter 8 problems such as these by using actual schedules which incorporate examples of mistakes, but before doing this we must also consider the problems which arise from lack of understanding of the question. In a survey on shopping which I made a few years ago one of my student interviewers was questioning an old lady about the grocer's shop she used. The survey was a comparison between self-service and counter-service grocers and the student was puzzled that the old lady claimed to shop at a counter-service yet all her answers suggested that she used a self-service shop. In the end the student asked the lady if she really did mean that her grocer was a counter-service and the old lady replied, 'Oh yes, it's counter-service all right. All the things are out on counters and you go round helping yourself.' Fortunately this was in a pilot survey and the warning was heeded in the survey proper.

One difficulty about questioning is the one of leading the respondent towards a particular response. If people are asked 'Would you like . . .', there is a good chance that they will say yes. Although the question may seem clumsier for it, it is absolutely necessary to give a genuine choice, and even though it may sound stilted to ask, 'Do you approve or disapprove of . . .' at least this presents a fair choice. For examples of carefully worded questions in public opinion polls it is worth looking at the regular publication of the Gallup Poll, which is entitled the Gallup Political Index.

A further regular pitfall in framing questions is the double question. This is very often to be spotted by the word 'and' linking two separate items. For example the question 'Would you like to become a doctor and work in a hospital?' is a double question because the respondent might like to become a doctor, but not work in a hospital. This is an obvious example, but more subtle ones crop up frequently and they indicate that the designer has thought only of asking the question, not trying to answer it.

A great deal of faulty question phrasing stems from the survey worker being over-involved in his own ideas. Often the survey is to be conducted after months of work on a theme, and by this time the researcher has become very immersed in the work and tends to forget that other people do not have his interest or knowledge. For reasons such as this it is important to ensure that the 'final edition' of the interview schedule has been adequately gone over and tried out before it is used in the full scale field survey. I suggest that there are a number of steps which should be gone through towards this end.

Testing of Interview Schedules

The important fact about a field survey is that it is a once-and-for-all social situation which cannot be re-created. It is no use realising at an analysis stage that Question 3 is really ambiguous and all the respondents should be asked it again in a different way. I doubt if any survey has ever been carried out without the researcher having some regrets at the analysis stage about some questions which could have been handled better, but the good researcher makes sure in advance that these regrets are as few as possible. I suggest that the regrets can be reduced by using the following steps.

(1) Pre-pilot open interviews
(2) Roughing-out questions and layout
(3) Internal testing
(4) Pilot survey
(5) Survey proper

These five steps are obviously a counsel of perfection, but most surveys can cope to some degree with them. The pre-pilot open interviews will be conducted with a small sub-sample of the population concerned and will, in the earliest stages, be as much hypothesis-seeking as anything else. But this stage is vitally important for the researcher to get the feel of the situation. In many instances of sociological research the research worker is to survey a group of people who are quite different from himself. He may be working among old people, or schoolchildren or even convicts. To start framing questions without first having talked to some of the people concerned about his ideas would be ludicrous.

Having carried out such interviews (and no set limit to them can be laid down) the researcher may then make a start on his topic headings and detailed questions. It is virtually certain that he will require details of the personal characteristics of his informants, in many cases such facts as sex, age, marital status, social class, educational level and so on. These details are often called 'classificatory data' since they form one part of much classification of other questions. For example, distinctions often need to be made between the opinions of men and women, single women and married women, young people and old people. Classificatory data provide one side of the subsequent table for analysis purposes. Even at the early stage of enquiry it may well be possible to decide what actual classifications will be used for these data. Male and female is simple. Marital status will probably suffice with single, married, widowed and 'any other' unless the survey is particularly concerned with divorced or legally separated people. Social class may well be based upon the occupation of the male head of the household according to a predetermined scale, such as the Registrar-General's, or the Institute of Practitioners in Advertising. There may be problems of deciding the social class of women, but these will have to be settled at some time. Educational level will probably be analysed by the last educational institution attended full-time in some hierarchical fashion, or by the actual educational attainments of the informant. It is worth noting here that the spread of comprehensive secondary education will eventually make the old simple division between secondary modern and grammar a redundant form of analysis. Age may be classified according to any set of categories deemed to be useful for the purpose in hand. Obviously five year categories will be more discriminating, but they may be unnecessarily small grades. A ten year age group is more likely to be useful, but the actual category limits should be carefully thought about. It may be attractive to use 20–29 as a category, but if there is any importance in the study attached to distinguishing between adults and minors obviously 21 must be a cut-off point. There might be more advantage in making the categories run mid-way across the ten-year groups, giving 25 to 34 as a group if it is felt that some significant changes take place in people's lives in their mid-thirties, or other points in the mid-sections of the decades. This class certainly helps to end some older people at the age of general retirement. Obviously all age-groups are arbitrary; the point being made here is that the actual divisions used should be chosen for their usefulness in classifying people for the purposes of the research being undertaken, and this decision should be considered at an early stage.

The topics themselves will probably be reasonably apparent after the pre-pilot interview stage and two decisions need to be made at the layout stage. Firstly, what order should the topics be in, and secondly what questions should be asked under each topic heading? Let us suppose for the moment that the survey is concerned with leisure activities and is a comparison between social classes. Obviously the classificatory data will give special attention to the factor of social class and also to such important variables as age, sex, marital status and so on. The topic headings might then discriminate between leisure activities within the home, individual and collective; leisure activities outside the home, organised and unorganised, and use of commercial leisure facilities. These five possible areas of leisure activities are only illustrative for the particular methodological problem here being discussed, they are not in fact derived from any research, but they will suffice to show that the researcher would now be able to think in what order they might be placed so as to give a sensible progression in an interview situation. It might well be that the researcher decided to start inside the home with individual activities, and lead on to collective ones. Then he might move to outside the home taking unorganised ones first before organised ones, and then conclude with commercial leisure. The point here is that the order of topics would then, we hope, seem sensible *to the informant*. It is very important indeed that the informant be considered at the earliest possible stage since he or she will be doing the work of supplying answers to the questions and a good 'flow' in the interview will help greatly in establishing and maintaining interest and rapport.

Under each topic heading the actual questions themselves will be placed. Some people like to use a card for each question at this stage so that it is simple to move questions about as it seems desirable to order and re-order them for the best sequence. At this stage the actual response categories may not have been considered in detail, but if the questions themselves justify inclusion some thought should have been given to the response categories envisaged for analysis since it is the *answers* which will be analysed. Nevertheless, the questions themselves, at this stage, will be the main focus, and also at this stage we might allow more questions to be included than are likely to be used at the final stage. When they are all put together under topic headings the full interview schedule will then tell us how long the interview is likely to take and if it is much too big pruning can be undertaken at once. The writing stage, when topics and questions are actually put down, can be quite a salutary experience. What seemed to be a simple matter when merely held as a mental question, verbally unframed and with no thought given to response, appears as a simply impossible problem when it has actually to be put down on paper. We may, for example, think to ourselves that it would be very useful to ask a housewife if she works outside the house at all, and this sounds easy enough in our heads. But as soon

I

as we have to commit this question to paper we discover (or we certainly *should* discover) that this is a difficult question to ask clearly, and so far as the possible answers are concerned there seems to be no end to what replies we may receive and how to categorise them seems a nightmare.

At this stage then we may only be roughing-out our interview schedule, but the more attention we can give to detail at this stage the more we are likely to be saving ourselves trouble later on. Decisions to put off until a later stage the actual wording or analysis categories can often be rationalised as being safeguards against too rigid a mental outlook on what may be a very exploratory field of research. But there are numerous instances which come to my mind of research in which all the problems of analysis were left until the survey had been done and then anything up to, or even over, a year, was needed to sort out the tangled mass of answers to vague questions. This may have its attractions to people who enjoy solving such problems and who have the time for it, but much of this work is not necessary if fore-thought is used at the planning stage.

When a draft schedule has been produced the next stage is what has been referred to previously as 'internal testing'. This means trying the schedule out, *not* on a sample of people for whom it is intended in its final version, but on people who are probably one's colleagues at work; that is, people who are likely to know something about survey work itself and schedule design. The point of this stage is that it is cheap and easy, and does not necessitate going outside the building. But the results can be absolutely invaluable if one's colleagues look over the draft and, without any holds barred, pick on every doubtful point. I can recall some years ago at this stage that a young postgraduate student who was designing a schedule containing a lot of attitude questions had his schedule internally tested by a number of people and practically every question he had put was a double one. Had he gone out with the schedule the results would have been chaotic, yet he himself had not seen these double features until they were pointed out to him at the internal testing stage. Probably the most valuable thing about this stage is that the schedule compiler gets a sort of 'consumers' view' for the first time. A commonplace fault amongst schedule designers is not thinking enough about what it is like to be on the receiving end of the questions. If he is brave enough to try his draft out on critical, expert colleagues he can be reasonably sure that what emerges at the end will be rid of double questions, ambiguities, leading questions and so on, and his helpful colleagues, in pretending to be informants, will also probably have thought up some difficult answers for him to classify too. All in all, this is a valuable stage which researchers who do not accept criticism very easily will probably wish to avoid, but if they do consciously and deliberately avoid it, they have only themselves to blame for not taking advantage of a most useful step in schedule preparation.

After the mauling received from his dear colleagues the designer eventually produces what seems to be a document which meets most internal criticisms. It next goes to a small sample of the real consumers for test. This is the stage of the 'dress rehearsal' or pilot.

Views on the function of the pilot stage vary amongst research workers, but I view the pilot stage as being the last one before the actual survey itself and therefore a stage where, as far as possible, the interview schedule is near to its final form in both questions and answer categories. I see little value in the interview schedule going into the field to a small sub-sample of respondents if the designer knows in advance that there is a lot of work still to be done. If this work is apparent it seems only sensible to do it and *then* try out as good a schedule as one can produce on the real people. After all, the survey will have to be done at some stage and it is only going to be helpful to carry out a pilot if it tells the designer something he did not know. There is little to be gained in trying out something which he knows already to be inadequate. In my view the importance of the pilot stage is that it confronts the, perhaps, over-sophisticated schedule with down-to-earth respondents. By this is meant that the designer, and his colleagues, may be *too* expert, too sophisticated, too used to jargon, too well educated and able to verbalise. And in addition they will all understand the purpose of the survey. The respondents, in a normal population, will contain much larger numbers of unsophisticated, poorly educated, inarticulate and non-jargon-using ordinary people whose task it will be to try to answer questions, some of which may be quite baffling to them. The pilot survey should be the essential stage at which the surveyor is forced to come down from his ivory tower and make himself communicate with his sample of respondents. It is at the pilot stage that 'stuffiness' in the wording of questions becomes very apparent. Questions may look all right on paper simply because we accept a more formal style in writing than we do in speech, but sound absolutely frightful when put into speech. A simple example will suffice; many people in writing use the word 'commence' rather than 'begin'. In a written question it would be possible to ask, 'In what year did you commence secondary education?' Just try saying that sentence out loud and see how pompous and unnatural it sounds. A further small point; we often try to avoid ending written sentences with a preposition if we remember our training at school. But the above sentence, apart from replacing 'commence' by 'begin', *sounds* more natural if we do in fact end it with the preposition. Try saying out loud, 'What year did you begin your secondary education in?' This, surely, is much more what we really would say in a normal conversation.

One further point about the pilot stage is its value in helping problems of analysis. The response categories are just as important as the questions at this stage, and even a relatively small number of responses can help in re-drafting response categories. We may find that a particular reply which we had expected to be only very occasionally given looks as if it might well be much more prevalent than we had expected. We might, for example, find that in a particular residential area there are unexpectedly large numbers of households with 'lodgers' and so we might want to add this as a specific category in the household composition: or we might find that on an attitude question views are rather more extreme than we had anticipated and so a new response category could be usefully put in to save us noting responses under 'Others specify . . .' in many cases.

When the lessons from the pilot survey have been fully learned alterations will be made where necessary, but if the work done prior to the pilot has been adequate the alterations consequent upon the pilot should not be great. Indeed it could be regarded as a measure of the previous work how little needs doing after the pilot. But when all has been considered the next and final step is the survey itself. This involves a number of considerations and these will be dealt with under separate headings. Perhaps the most general point to be made about the survey proper is that it should be regarded as an end-point to be reached after careful preparation. Whatever mistakes are made in the survey will be irrevocable. A poor response rate cannot be botched over. A badly phrased question cannot be re-worded after the survey is complete. Everything that can be done in preparation for the survey should therefore be done; there is precious little that can be done afterwards without distorting the reality of the survey. Alterations made afterwards have a tendency to show; those which do not show may be examples of dishonesty by the surveyor.

Surveys vary enormously in their nature according to the purpose of the enquiry and the sample of informants approached. The problems encountered in a survey of old people living in old people's homes will obviously be different from those encountered in trying to interview a representative sample of ordinary adolescents. We are not here concerned with the problems involved in obtaining samples,[2] our focus is on the survey once the sample has been decided on and drawn. For the sake of convenience in discussing problems of surveying we will use the ordinary house-to-house survey as the general case for discussion.

Contacting Informants

One of the basic problems in surveying is to obtain a good response from one's informants. When we discuss the use of self-completed questionnaires this will be a special point of detail, but it can be a major problem in interview surveys also. In a survey of a 'closed' institution such as a prison or a firm, the informants may be instructed to co-operate with interviewers because of agreement about the survey by the people in authority, but in many instances of samples from the general population no such authority exists and the surveyor must try to obtain co-operation as best he can by interesting his informants in the survey and gaining their completely freely-given co-operation. What is surprising is how very generously this co-operation is given in many cases. Market research firms, B.B.C.

<hr>

[2] See M. Schofield: *The Sexual Behaviour of Young People*, London, 1965, for an interesting account of the problems involved in sampling young people.

audience research, the Central Office of Information Social Survey Division and many other agencies all depend for the bulk of their success on the co-operation of the public. Much interviewing is done for this type of work simply by approaching people in the street, or by knocking on people's doors at home.

Personal Approach

Let us consider what the interviewer is trying to do when he seeks an interview and what the reaction of the informant may be. The interviewer is seeking to interview a sample of housewives on an estate about, let us say, the work-day pattern of wives who work only within the home. The sample has been based on a random sample of houses. The interviewer wants (a) to find out if the informant is a full-time housewife and (b) if yes, how she spends her working day. If the woman is in the right category he wants to ask her a whole list of questions about her life. On the other hand, the housewife, engaged in her working day, hears a knock on the door and finds a complete stranger there with a chip-board to which is attached a rather large sheet (or sheets) of paper covered with duplicated sentences and ominous boxes. Let us try to consider, from both sides, what is needed to move from this original confrontation to a successfully completed interview.

The interviewer (let us say it is a man for, ease of being able to say 'he' and 'she' in this case, even though most interviewers are women) will expect to open the conversation and he has the task of explaining to the housewife, simply and briefly:

    (a) Where he is from (the sponsoring body)
    (b) What he is doing (the purpose of the survey)
    (c) Why the housewife was chosen in the sample
    (d) Why she should grant the interview.

Looking at it from the housewife's point of view her phrasing of these points would be:

    (a) Who are you and where are you from?
    (b) What do you want?
    (c) Why choose me to help you?
    (d) Why should I help you anyway?

If dealt with in this order the opening gambit would be 'I am an interviewer from the North Midlands Institute for Sociological Research and we are carrying out a survey of the working-day of housewives. Your house has come up in a random sample of houses in this area and, if you are a full-time housewife, we would like you to tell us about your working day since we believe that a survey of this subject would be of great value in helping all housewives.'

In the above passage points (a) and (b) are easier to explain than points (c) and (d). Point (c), on sampling, is a technical matter which is very difficult to explain properly and it would be beyond the abilities of most housewives to understand what random, or any other sort of, sampling means. But fortunately most people who are asked to help in surveys are prepared to accept that they are appropriate people to answer questions on the survey for which they are approached, and particularly where people feel that they are being asked to give 'expert' information this can be seen as rather a compliment. . . . 'If you want to know about how a housewife organises her day *I* can tell you everything you need to know.' But whilst people in the sample *can* give the information, the question still has to be answered as to *why* they should bother. In most cases the reasonable answer will be along the lines that those people who give information to the survey will be contributing to an overall study, the results of which will be useful for a better understanding by everyone of the general problem and also will specially help specialists who might be interested in (in this case) the housewife's day. These specialists might be architects, furniture manufacturers, social workers, magazine publishers, domestic equipment manufacturers, shopkeepers—all the people who are affected by the housewife's day. The fictitious example being used here is not the easiest one to explain to an informant, but many much more difficult ones have been explained and interviews obtained.

Approach by Letter

One possible way of getting round the problem of the 'door step' explanation is to write a letter to people in the sample to let them know in advance of the survey and the coming call by an interviewer. One advantage of a letter is that all the points (a) to (d) above can be dealt with in advance and so the interviewer is expected and time is saved in not having to go through all the verbal explanation. In some cases, especially amongst people of higher status, the letter is regarded as a more polite way of asking for the interview and it helps differentiate the interviewer, when he calls, from marauding salesmen. As against the use of a letter it must be noted that it is not easy to write a short but very clear letter explaining completely what the informant may want to know, and if the recipient decides that she (or he) does not want to co-operate then she is warned in advance of the interviewer's call. If she is determined not to be interviewed she could even write back and say quite clearly 'keep away', in which case no earnest explanation by the interviewer is possible. There is also the danger with using a letter that people may misread it—or just look at it and not read it properly. I have myself been welcomed as a local council surveyor come to look at houses in a slum area, and I had an assistant who was once received as a person who was trying to recruit voluntary social workers. These instances arose because the recipients just did not read the letters sent to them. Lastly, of course, sending a letter to a large sample does involve more costs than just knocking at doors, but the proportionate cost of a letter, when looked at against the total cost of an interview, is very small.

If a letter is to be used, a few basic details should be observed. Firstly the recipient must have the name of the organisation given quite clearly, and the status of the signator should be given also. The recipient has the right to know who is writing from where; letters from private addresses and statusless persons carry no weight. In explaining the survey and its value, the letter should be brief and at such a level as to interest and convince the recipient. This does not mean writing down' to people, but it does mean being clear and non-technical. The appeal is, after all, asking a personal favour of the recipient. If the letter can actually be addressed by name to the intended respondent it will carry more weight than any address such as 'The Occupant' or 'The Housewife', which is likely to be opened with the expectation of it being advertising or political literature.

But whatever method of entrée may be used, the interviewer is the vital person so far as the actual interview is concerned.

The Interview

The qualities required of interviewers will vary greatly according to the complexities of interview schedules used and also the degree of informality permitted in the interviews. In academic, exploratory research where the results are not to be analysed and presented in statistical fashion a research worker may feel that he cannot have any assistant helping with interviews since his whole approach is so subjective and non-statistical. But as soon as results are presented in tabular form it does seem reasonable to suppose that there is sufficient uniformity of approach to have allowed for more than one interviewer, and, of course, for subsequent repetition of the interviews so as to replicate the enquiry. Wherever there appears to be a 'mystique' about the interviewing, suggestions that these results were possible because of some mystical skills possessed by the interviewer, then one is likely to be moving from sociology towards journalism, or special pleading at the very least. Interviewing is certainly a skilled job when carried out properly, but it is not a mystical union between interviewer and respondent. Obviously some people make better interviewers than others, but with reasonable training no normal person who is reasonably able to carry on a conversation should find it impossible to undertake interviews. Hundreds of ordinary women are highly competent interviewers, and a glance at some of the very complex interview schedules used by market research firms and the government Social Survey show that they are capable of carrying out very intricate interviews which would probably be beyond the capabilities of many untrained academics!

The ideal schedule is one which can be used by a team of interviewers and yield the same stimuli to informants with their responses being recorded in the same way. The survey interview therefore requires expertise, not 'flair' on the interviewer's part. This does not mean that the interviewer becomes a cold clinical robot, but it does mean that he or she uses a particular instrument in the way that it is designed to be used—for objective study. The interviewer who changes questions, who adds bits to questions, who generally messes about with the schedule is not being clever, she is being a bad technician.

All interviewers should, wherever possible, be carefully briefed about the schedule they are about to use, and wherever possible a 'guide to interviewers' should accompany, or be incorporated with, the schedule.. Where interviewers are centrally grouped they can be called together for a briefing session where any queries can be raised and dealt with on the spot, but where large organisations have interviewers scattered about the country this may be a counsel of perfection, although peripatetic field-work supervisors can do invaluable work in this as well as other functions.

Interviewers must seek out, contact and interview their allotted sub-samples, and once they have been given their tasks they must work relatively independently. In the case of street interviews where they may be working on 'quota' samples (so many people of certain sex, age and class categories chosen by the interviewer to fit into the required quota) the discretion allowed may be quite great. The temptation to 'fiddle' quotas or interviews is always present, and for an interviewer who is not getting interviews this temptation must at times be great. Nevertheless the whole basis of survey work is one of trust and relatively few interviewers abuse this trust. What is important here is sporadic checking of results, with internal checks on results and occasional calls back to houses to check that interviews have been made. Also, after interviews have been made, interviewers must check their schedules for errors of recording, omissions or any other faults, and good supervision will again see that this is done.

The ultimate aim of the interviewer is to produce a well completed schedule for every interview assigned to her. The ability to win over an informant who is undecided whether or not to grant the interview is important, as is the ability to put people at their ease and reassure them that the interview is not going to be some sort of *viva voce* examination. These are the human skills of the interviewer which will obtain good interviews without over assisting the informants. At the end of an interview the informant will be thanked for co-operating and left feeling satisfied after what was an interesting and worthwhile discussion. But apart from having the qualities of tact, the interviewer will also have qualities of accuracy, since the results of the interviews will go, on the schedules, to other people, office staff, whose task will be analysis.

Before considering problems of analysis we will next make a parallel study of the problems involved in the use of self-completed questionnaires. When this is done the common problems of analysis can be dealt with.

7

The Self-Completed Questionnaire

Introduction

In contrast to the interview schedule which is used by the interviewer as an *aide memoire* and which is completed by the interviewer, the questionnaire is normally completed without a research worker being present at all; the informant has written instructions before him and fills in the questionnaire himself. This description of the questionnaire is, however, a generalised one, and questionnaires vary quite a lot in the way they are administered. Perhaps the best known example of a questionnaire sent by post is the income tax form which all tax payers receive each year requiring complete details to be given of income and certain expenditure. Another famous questionnaire is the one used in the decennial census of population. This questionnaire is delivered to each dwelling by a census officer (usually a local government official) and collected by him a few days later. Whilst the census questionnaire contains an enormous amount of helpful instructions for its completion, the census officer may also give help to respondents if they are still baffled by it. Some questionnaires may be distributed to a particular group of people who are together in a particular place, and instructions for completing the questionnaire may then be mainly verbal. Two instances of this kind are a census of church attendance in which I was once involved in which the vicar gave the instructions for each question to the congregation, and another example in that of market research trials of advertising films for television, where housewives are invited to a cinema, given questionnaires for their comments on the 'commercials' and then told how to fill them in by the master of ceremonies on the stage. Many forms which we fill in are questionnaires of a sort; every student who registers for the coming session at university each October probably fills in a number of forms which are questionnaires of a type (often a very poor type).

For the purposes of this chapter we will concentrate on the questionnaire which is circulated through the post, since this is the most commonplace use of this particular technique for collecting information. The problems arising from this will be considered under two headings—the respondents and the information to be collected.

The Respondents

One of the great attractions of the postal questionnaire enquiry is the ease and cheapness which it seems to have. Rather than having to spend many hours, at high cost, in sending out interviewers armed with interview schedules to locate and talk to informants, all one need do is knock out a list of questions, have them duplicated, put the whole lot in an envelope addressed to the informant (with a self-addressed envelope enclosed) and then wait for the Post Office and the recipients to do all the work. In theory this sounds so delightful that it is surprising anyone considers interviews worth bothering with at all. In fact, with the increasing popularity of sociology and quasi-sociology, it is unfortunately true that far too many questionnaires are sent out these days. Education authorities, in particular, have been inundated with education students' questionnaires and have been forced to put a ban on all surveys other than those, normally for higher degrees, which have been carefully vetted by the appropriate officers.

Voluntary organisations, some of good repute, but others of little standing in the community, have been caught in the thralls of this new game, and even official research bodies themselves seem now to have the questionnaire bug and produce what are probably the longest and most complicated questionnaires of the lot. It is almost as if the Post Office slogan had been misprinted and read 'Someone, somewhere is waiting for a questionnaire from you'. Why should this form of research be so popular?

There are a number of reasons. Firstly, it is possible to send out a very large number of questionnaires quite cheaply. Paper costs very little, and even with increasing postal charges the total cost of questionnaire, two envelopes and two stamps would still come to much less than a shilling. So to send out 1,000 questionnaires would cost under £50, and if you have the nerve to send an *unstamped* reply envelope the cost would be under £25. Coupled with the 'broadcast' method of sending out questionnaires is the commonplace habit of only being concerned with *numbers* of replies and not *proportions*. If a large enough number is sent out then even a low *proportion* of replies gives a *number* which looks impressive. If this number is analysed then results can still look good. An example taken from a report in *New Society*[1] will illustrate this point. The North West London group of the Abortion Law Reform Association sent out 'more than 2,000 questionnaires' to doctors on the London medical list; 750 (about 35 per cent) were returned and these were analysed. *Of the respondents*, three quarters said yes to hospital abortions in the first twelve weeks of pregnancy on the N.H.S. But if we take the total number of medical practitioners *asked* as being 2,000 (and the extract said 'more than 2,000') then 75 per cent of 750 becomes only 28 per cent of 2,000—a rather different way of putting things. Similarly whilst 84 per cent of the 750 said that abortion was a safe operation for a woman in good health, this becomes only 32 per cent of 2,000.

This example is not at all concerned with the rights or wrongs of abortions, we are merely using it to show how attractive the results of a postal questionnaire survey can look if one does not look closely enough. The most significant fact of the above survey is that the response rate was no higher than 35 per cent yet the surveyors in presenting their results ignored the 65 per cent of people who did not reply. Tables which said in every case 'non-response=65 per cent' would not be very impressive.

Non-response, then, is one of the greatest of problems in postal questionnaire surveys, and it is necessary to consider it from a number of angles. Firstly we will consider why postal surveys should be useful, secondly for what sort of respondents they are particularly useful, and thirdly what can be done to get a maximum response from them.

Although questionnaires must have their limitations in the data they can collect (as we shall discuss later) the attraction of saving in costs of interviews makes a postal enquiry attractive at first glance.

[1] 25th February, 1965.

Yet it must be recognised that the limitations are very real. To send a postal questionnaire to a *general* sample of the population would not be likely to result in a very good response, and the response one did get would inevitably contain biases of some sort. Suppose that we were trying to find out how people spend their leisure time, and a general sample of all sorts of people was desirable. To send out a questionnaire to all ages and classes might seem reasonable at first glance, but our hopes of a good response would probably be dashed by non-response. This can be considered in a number of ways.

Firstly, many people would not be in the slightest bit interested in our survey, and, not having the persuasive interviewer to tell them why the survey is so important, they would just throw the questionnaire away. These people *could* complete it, but they *will not*.

Secondly, some people unused to receiving postal enquiries of this sort will feel that this all too complicated for them, they will not be able to understand why the survey is being done, or how the answers should be given, so they will throw it away too. These people might respond verbally to an interviewer, but the written document is beyond them. They *cannot*.

The 'cannots' will include the illiterates and the near-illiterates of our society, and will thus cut off a section of the lower intelligence levels, resulting in some bias towards the higher intelligence levels. But the 'will nots' are likely to be just as important in the non-response, since they are the people who just don't see why they should give their time and energy to filling in these damn fool questions that have just landed out of the blue onto the breakfast table from some organisation they have never heard of before in their lives. People with a wide range of interests, who take a lively interest in the society in which they live, may be expected to be favourably predisposed to filling in questionnaires, but how many people can we expect to find in this category? And how representative are they anyway of the general mass of the population? It therefore looks as if a *general* sample would give us a bias towards livelier, literate, more intelligent people. We should also expect, *a priori*, that we would get a better response from people who did have an interest already in the subject of our enquiry. Mothers of small children living in the area of a criminal lunatic asylum might well be more favourably disposed to answering a questionnaire on attitudes to the treatment of criminals than women who had never had children living in an area where there are no prisons within miles. Interest, particularly self-interest, is a conducive factor towards completing questionnaires. It is therefore useful to consider the questionnaire as a tool for a survey of particular people who may be assumed to have a personal interest in the subject of the enquiry.

A questionnaire sent to members of a professional association from their own headquarters on a matter of vital interest to them all should obtain a good response, particularly if the topic is one on which there are fairly strong views on two sides. A questionnaire enquiry sent to people who are themselves involved in a matter should gain a good response. An enquiry about the problems of wastage amongst women teachers is both of importance and interest to the women involved. In this instance, which was actually studied by R. K. Kelsall,[2] a response rate of 84 per cent was achieved.

A further point may suggest itself from some of the examples noted above. Although it might, for some questions, be desirable to interview women teachers, they are a group who are not all to be found conveniently located in one area of the country. Indeed, for any particular group of women teachers trained at a particular time, a certain proportion are quite likely to have left this country altogether. The postal questionnaire (so long as addresses can be traced) enables the surveyor to get in touch with the sample no matter where they may be, so long as postal services can reach them. Part of the women teachers enquiry was devoted to tracing respondents by sending lists of names to women trained together and asking if they still had contact with each other. Tracing the location of sample members can be a very intricate and frustrating process, but once this is done the respondents can be contacted anywhere in the world.

Looking at the question of the respondents then, it is clear that the postal questionnaire enquiry is best suited to rather special groups of people who are likely to be widely dispersed geographically. We may now consider some of the problems involved in the actual information to be collected.

[2] R. K. Kelsall: *Women and Teaching*, H.M.S.O., London, 1963.

The Information

Sidney and Beatrice Webb give a good example of how not to construct a questionnaire in their *Methods of Social Study*. A questionnaire they devised for sending to trade unions would probably have taken a dozen men a dozen years to complete, if they could indeed have managed to complete it at all. No questionnaire which is daunting to the beholder is likely to produce much enthusiasm, and whilst interviewees may be carried along by the social relationships established in the talk of an interview, the questionnaire respondent who looks through twenty pages of closely printed questions alone is hardly to be expected to thrill in anticipation. No questionnaire which is too long and involved can be expected to have a favourable reception, and the limitations of the method must be accepted. In the interview a particular topic can be made the focus of a number of questions without seeming to be too prying so long as the informant is interested in the topic itself. But if a questionnaire attempts the same amount of 'probing' (to use the technical term) it is likely to look both over complicated and probably too inquisitive. A skilled interviewer can cope with a large number of, often personal, questions with all sorts of instructions as to which questions to follow on with if particular answers are given, and which questions to drop in particular cases. The respondent in the well conducted interview is made to feel this is all very simple by the skill of the interviewer. In the questionnaire situation however the skill is in the layout of the questionnaire itself and in the recipient as to how well he can handle the questions. The difference is a very important one indeed and has basic effects on the limits of the questionnaire.

As a general principle the interview is likely to be most suitable for questions seeking 'depth', whilst the questionnaire (particularly on large samples) is likely to get breadth of coverage on reasonably straightforward questions. To assist the respondent in completing a questionnaire, and this should always be one of the questionnaire designer's prime aims, pre-set answers are helpful. It is simpler to tick in a box, or ring round a word or phrase than it is to write in one's own answer, and this is likely to make for easier analysis too. But including pre-set answers takes up space on the questionnaire, so that

K

a balance must be held here. The whole problem of questionnaire enquiries is how far one can go with the questionnaire, and how much one can anticipate the reactions of the respondents. What looks to the designer to be a useful set of responses, all there to help the respondent, may look to the respondent to be a daunting set of complicated phrases and boxes. What may be thought to be a help may in fact be a hindrance, and it must always be remembered that for better or worse (and it may well be for worse) the respondent sees the *whole* of the questionnaire at one go. There is no way of feeding questions to him one by one as in an interview. If he is put off by the size or appearance of the questionnaire he is lost to the survey before he starts answering. He may also, of course, get so far with the answers and then decide he has had enough part way through, a situation which rarely occurs in an interview. It is clear that to get a response from the recipient of the questionnaire, he must be made to feel that the whole business is worth doing, and for this the instructions and appeal which precede the questions themselves are of paramount importance. We will call this section the 'covering letter' since it is, so often, written in the form of a letter from the surveyor.

The Covering Letter

Whilst a person to be interviewed can be initially approached by letter and then later followed up with the actual interview, such a separation is hardly feasible for a postal questionnaire enquiry. In this case the introduction and the collection of the information must be done together, and the introduction must cover many of the matters dealt with by the interviewer in initiating the interview. These matters may be considered as ways of dealing with possible questions raised by the recipient of the questionnaire.

What is this circular letter and set of questions about? The covering letter must, very quickly and simply, tell the recipient *what* is being surveyed. Fancy jargon and long words will not help here. A direct and simple explanation is needed.

Why is this survey being carried out? Here a reasonable explanation of the value of the survey is necessary to convince the recipient that this is a job worth helping in. If the survey can clearly be related to some burning issue of the day all the better.

Why ask *me* to help you? Here some very brief explanation of how the recipient came to be included in the sample is required. Since some form of random sampling has probably been used this part can be used to stress the need for a good response rate.

Why should *I* give my time to answering all these questions? To answer this the surveyor can point out that if all the recipients reply they will be contributing information and views which, when analysed, will be of value for whatever group or institution is relevant.

What will happen to my questionnaire if I do fill it in? This question requires the conventional guarantee of anonymity and an assurance that all questionnaires will eventually be destroyed after analysis.

It can be seen that a covering letter which deals simply and clearly and *briefly* with the above points must be carefully constructed. A further point which is very relevant is that the recipient must know from where the survey is being carried out. Headed notepaper is customarily used by research organisations, but it is sensible and courteous for the covering letter to be signed wherever possible and to have below the signature the typed name of the signator and the status he holds in the organisation. Not only does this make the appeal seem more personal, but it also enables the recipient to have a real live person to whom he can write if he has any queries to raise about the survey. If the letter is separate from the actual questionnaire itself the recipient can retain it after returning the completed questionnaire and he thus has some tangible record of the event.

Facilitating Replies

A good covering letter is obviously one of the basic factors in questionnaire work. But other things can be done to help get a good response rate.

It is grossly impertinent to send a questionnaire by post and to expect the recipient to pay the return postage. Some even worse cases do occur where the recipient does not even receive an addressed envelope; in these cases the sender does not deserve to get a single reply. When people are asked to fill in questionnaires they are being asked to give some time and quite often a fair amount of mental energy for a task which will benefit them personally very little, and the end product of which they may never see. It must be appreciated then that the respondents are doing a great favour to the researcher, and they must not be expected to incur one halfpenny of costs in doing this. It is therefore quite essential that questionnaires be accompanied by stamped addressed envelopes which will be used for the return of the completed questionnaire.

There is sometimes a financial saving to be had in large surveys by using special envelopes which indicate that postage will be paid by the recipient. This method of 'Business Reply Service' is done under licence from the Post Office and is very commonly used in commercial advertising. For this reason it is somewhat suspect for use in sociological research. The recipient knows that postage will only be paid if the envelope is used: if it is not used the postage is not paid. But if the envelope actually has a real postage stamp on it the recipient is made aware that the sender is prepared to take a risk in using a stamp. I always feel that the Reader's Digest Association are clever in using actual stamps in preference to the business reply method, since this must surely get them more replies—even though many of these replies are probably simply saying 'no' to their offers. In a sociological survey, which is *not* a commercial operation, the use of a real postage stamp is not only a demonstration of the 'risk' that the researcher is prepared to make, it is rather more a courteous gesture to the recipient which in effect says that an answer really is expected, and answers sent by post need stamps. Discourteous recipients may still steam the stamps off and use them for themselves, but if they do then they are in a poor moral position to criticise questionnaire surveys!

A great problem in sending out postal questionnaires is to decide what to do about following up people who do not reply. A close check should always be kept on the dates when the questionnaires go out. All questionnaires must have some identifying marks on them, even if they are only serial numbers, otherwise a questionnaire which did not ask for a recipient's name will be unidentifiable. (This is not such an obvious point—I do know of one postal survey in which the sender was so keen to observe anonymity that names and addresses were very explicitly *not* asked for and with no serial numbers the surveyor then had no idea who had replied and who had not). If all the questionnaires for a survey go out in one batch there is no particular problem; if they go out on several dates then records of posting dates should be kept separately.

After the questionnaires have been posted there will be a slight lapse of time before the first replies come trickling in. The trickle will then, one hopes, become a stream before it gradually declines to a trickle again. It is at some point when the trickle seems to be drying up that a follow-up must be considered. No hard and fast rule as to how many days should elapse after the post can be given. Some questionnaires may be much longer and more complicated than others, and thus be more likely to take time to complete. It is only likely to annoy recipients if they are reminded of their non-return before they have really had sufficient spare time to deal with them. On the other hand, the longer a person leaves the questionnaire undealt with, the less importance he is likely to attach to it, and there comes a point where it really does not seem worth bothering with *now*. The follow-up letter must come before the recipient has reached this 'point of no return' if one may be allowed such an execrable pun.

The actual wording of a follow-up letter must be carefully considered so that recipients are neither abused nor treated as idiots. The follow-up letter needs to be especially courteous and realise that the recipient may have been busy, but a good response rate *is* important and there is still time for the respondent to send back his completed questionnaire. It is a moot point as to whether it is worth sending a second copy of the questionnaire itself at this point. On balance this would seem to suggest that the recipient is a careless person who has managed to lose it in a relatively short period of time, and such an insinuation is rather presumptuous. After the initial sending out and the follow-up it is to be hoped that a good response will have been achieved, and that no more need be done. If the response has been poor in spite of the follow-up, a second follow-up might be considered, but this would be a strong indication of a failed survey. For a recipient to receive three requests from the researcher is going a bit far, and the person who has not responded to the first or second request is not very likely to respond to a third.

It would be a pleasant act of courtesy if all the people who return their questionnaires could receive postcards acknowledging receipt of the completed forms and thanking them for their co-operation. Unfortunately this is not likely to be possible since it could well add 50 per cent to the postal costs. Nevertheless if any public ways of acknowledging assistance given can be made they should be pursued. Since questionnaire surveys are often used on special groups or classes of people a few lines in, say, a professional journal likely to be read by them is one way of saying thank you. Local surveys are nearly always good for a few lines in the local newspaper and an indication of a satisfactory response can be given through this medium. I do not wish to labour the point, but surveyors *are* dependent on the goodwill of their respondents; to leave them feeling satisfied about the help they have given is common courtesy.

Designing Questionnaires

Since the problems of question formulation for questionnaires and interview schedules have so much in common we will leave details of the questions themselves for the next chapter. All that needs to be said here is that the general problems of design concerning questionnaires are much greater than those of designing schedules. The interview schedule is a technical device used by a trained person; if it looks like a cross between a railway timetable and a half-completed game of 'Battleships' this does not matter so long as the interviewer is helped in asking the right questions and recording the answers properly. By contrast, the questionnaire is likely to be extremely off-putting if it becomes such a complicated affair. In any questionnaire space is at a premium and for this reason the printed questionnaire has the advantage of getting more into a given space than a duplicated one and still looking uncrowded; this apart from the straightforward greater attraction of a printed document. Modern type face, particularly 'sans serif' gives a very clear image and can make a questionnaire aesthetically pleasing. In very large and expensive surveys it may be well worthwhile to take advice from a qualified artistic designer who can advise on layout and type-face. The only caution against these gentlemen is that sometimes they put art before utility, and I personally did not care for one questionnaire I saw where the designer had decided to banish all question marks on aesthetic grounds. I found the result decidedly difficult to read.

A last point to consider is that questionnaires nearly always have to be folded into envelopes and will receive a fair amount of man-handling before they are dealt with. A good quality paper is a good investment. Not only does the quality surface give a satisfactory appearance, but it means that by the time the document gets to the coders it will not just be a tattered wreck.

Now let us consider the art of asking questions.

8

How to Ask Questions

In the two previous chapters we have discussed some of the problems that arise in trying to ask the right question the right way, and in Chapter 6 we touched on some of the specific dangers which must be guarded against if questions are to be satisfactorily asked, answered and analysed. In this chapter we shall look at problems common to interview schedules and questionnaires in so far as points of detail are concerned. First of all we shall consider some of the specific issues to be dealt with, and then, using a dummy interview schedule which contains a large number of faults, we can try out our skill in a game of 'spot the blunder'.

Some General Points

Bowley's warning (noted in Chapter 6) against asking too many questions is a good starting point for any questionnaire or schedule designer. There is little point in asking respondents for information which is readily available from other sources. One is likely to want the sex of a respondent in most enquiries, but it would be disastrous to the success of an interview for the interviewer to ask this question of an informant (although in some studies of young people it might almost be necessary these days). Where observation is sufficient it is silly to verbalise a question. But questions can be avoided also in other situations. A survey of university students may well be done on a basis of a stratified sample in which the year of study, the faculty, the department, the sex and the age of the respondents are already known from actual records. In such a situation why ask for all the details from the respondents? It may be necessary for analysis purposes to have the details on each questionnaire, but this can be done easily by introducing a small box at the end, with symbols or abbreviations, headed 'For office use only'.

Of course, the criterion of relevance is fundamental to the inclusion of any questions. If the questionnaire designer does not know what use he is going to make of the replies when they are ready for analysis, it is pretty certain that he has ignored this particular point. It is easy enough to throw questions and answers away when you realise that you do not know how to analyse them, but this is a very wasteful procedure and hardly fair to one's respondents who have given time and energy to supplying answers.

Another problem of question asking is that questions can so easily get too complicated. When people are asked about their past history, with very detailed probing into their periods in particular jobs or times they lived in particular areas, there is a danger of asking respondents to try to work back to times they had practically forgotten about—and it may well be that the detail asked for is really not necessary at all for analysis. A question in an interview which requires the respondent to make a complicated calculation is likely to break the 'flow' of the interview; in a self-completed questionnaire it may result in the whole operation being brought to a close.

It is also dangerous to over-estimate the intelligence of one's respondents when asking questions. It is a very corny joke that expresses dismay at the fact that half our population is below average intelligence—and one has to know which average is being used to accept the statement ayway. But it must be remembered that in a *general* survey of the population the bulk of the respondents will be working class, not middle class, and many of them will not be very bright. It can therefore be both thoughtless and embarrassing to respondents if questions are asked which are beyond the grasp of the people in the sample. This danger can only be overcome by careful scrutiny of questions, and although it does not mean that the question designer should treat all his respondents as near imbeciles it does mean that the designer has to make himself aware that his own expertise and interest in the field of enquiry is not going to be found in his respondents.

Having made these general points which are common to both schedules and questionnaires, let us now look at points of detail, some of which have been touched on in Chapter 6.

Some Points of Detail

The question 'When did you stop beating your wife?' is probably the best-known example of a badly phrased question since it is based on an assumption which is probably not tenable in 99·9 per cent of cases. But whilst wife-beating is an obviously tricky area for question asking, other simpler areas still have their dangers. Without going into detail too much let us consider five problems of question asking and then try our hands on the 'spoof' interview schedule.

(1) Ambiguous questions. These are questions in which the phrasing results in the respondent being able to make more than one interpretation of the question. Few students need instruction in spotting the 'double entendre' in a lecture—as every lecturer knows well to his cost. It is a basic necessity in question framing that the question put shall have one meaning, and one meaning only, to all the respondents, no matter how many they may be.

(2) Leading questions. These are questions which, in the very way they are put, tend to influence the answer that a person gives. They are particularly important in attitude or opinion questions where a particular point at issue should always be presented from a central, or neutral starting point. To begin a question 'Do you agree that . . .' is to require a positive disagreement on the part of the respondent, and this is not an impartial way of presenting questions. Where there is an answer that can indicate yes/no or agree/disagree it is only fair to give the respondent on evenly balanced choice.

(3) Double questions. One might think that it is very easy to avoid double questions, since they must be obvious, but this is not always so. In trying to reduce the number of questions on a schedule or questionnaire, or in trying to save a small amount of space, the designer often thinks that an economy can be made by putting two questions together. The result is likely to be a double question which cannot be answered with one response. A simple example would be asking a person 'How often do you go to the cinema or theatre?' The answer is obviously so often to the cinema and so often to the theatre, but a *simple* answer to this one question could well be impossible and certainly if attempted would be virtually meaningless. Another common example might be to ask of a person with two

children 'How often do *they* go to the cinema?' Once again no one answer makes sense.

(4) Jargon and technical terms. Sociologists are often criticised, and often rightly criticised, for using jargon when plain English would make communication much easier. Perhaps this does not matter so much between sociologists if they are happy in coining new words for old actions, but for communication between sociologists and lay respondents the onus is always on the sociologist to find words which can be understood by his respondent; if he fails to do this he is being thoughtless and deserves a lack of response. It may be all right to talk to sociologists about 'kinship networks', but it is probably better to ask a working class housewife about her relatives. A questionnaire about work which asked a person if he 'holds an executive position' is likely to raise difficulties in analysis, since 'executive position' can be so very differently interpreted. Perhaps this second example is as much one of ambiguity as technicality, but whatever label one attaches to it, it is not a good question.

(5) Emotional questions. We have already noted that interviews and self-completed questionnaires depend on honest replies. One source of replies which may well not be honest is the question which gets the respondent emotionally involved. Question askers must take care in such delicate areas as sexual behaviour, religion, politics and social class especially. Where there are 'oughts' of behaviour in society, or a certain group within the society, respondents may well tend to give the answer which they think they 'ought' to give, rather than the answer which tells what they actually do. Thus questions on smoking, drinking, gambling and drug taking amongst young people (always depending on the circumstances under which questions are put) are always likely to result in replies which under-state reality. The person who is asked how many cigarettes a day he smokes is likely to give a figure on the low side rather than the high side, since cigarette smoking is dangerous to health, wasteful of money and often a nuisance to other people. It would be rather an act of defiance to over-state one's daily cigarette consumption. On the other hand if people are asked how many books they read a week, or month, or year, they are likely to over-state since book reading in most circles carries prestige rather than opprobrium. Now cigarette

smoking and book reading are not highly charged emotional areas, but they are nevertheless commonplace aspects of life about which 'oughts' may well have importance. A study of social mobility which asked a young graduate 'Do you think your father is of lower social class than yourself?' might well be very much to the heart of the matter under investigation, but it would be an extremely hard question to take without embarrassment. To ask a business man 'How often do you visit prostitutes when you are on business in London?' might throw an interesting light on managerial behaviour, but a very special type of interview would be needed for this sort of question. Emotions vary enormously amongst different people in different situations and it is hard to generalise about emotional questions. Perhaps the best advice in this section is to reiterate the previous advice to the question asker to try hard to think of the reaction likely from the respondent. Not to do this can lead to difficult situations.

A Practical Illustration

A few years ago my students were engaged with me on a survey into certain social aspects of local shopping. As part of the exercise all the students tried their hand at devising an interview schedule which was to be used for home interviews with people who did the main groceries shopping for the house. The various attempts contained, as first attempts always do, a good number of badly constructed questions. From these I put together, with very little embellishment of my own, the following interview schedule. It is full of errors of all sorts, and when I have gone through it with succeeding years of students we always seem to be able to add a few further faults which had not been noted before. I think one can practically go on for ever, depending upon how pernickety you want to be. No schedule or questionnaire is ever perfect and on points of fine detail there will always be room for personal disagreements as to how things could be improved. I suggest to the reader that you do not spend *too much* time on this 'spoof' schedule; it is mainly given here so that you can exercise your wits on spotting the grosser errors. When you have picked them out you will find a list given of the major ones. If you have found genuine errors of a gross type not mentioned in this list, give yourself a few bonus marks but don't go away feeling too smug —it is easy to tear other people's work to shreds, but probably not so easy to produce a first class alternative. If you don't think so, then I suggest you try your hand at re-phrasing all the bad questions you have criticised. The job of reconstruction will be a longer one than the job of demolition.

Shopping Survey

To Interviewers

Call at houses on your list and obtain interview with woman who does the principal shopping. Explain that you are from University Department of Sociology and that you are carrying out a survey into people's attitudes to counter-service and self-service grocers.

1. What is your age?   −20 ☐   20–30 ☐   30–40 ☐   40–50 ☐
                  50–60 ☐   60–70 ☐   70 and over ☐

2. What is your marital status?
        Married ☐   Single ☐   Widowed ☐

3. Have you any dependent children?   Yes/No
    If yes, how many?   1   2   3   4   5   6   7   or more

4. How long have you lived in this district?   …………years

5. Where do you buy your main groceries?
………………………………………………………………

6. Is it counter-service or self-service?
               S/S ☐   C/S ☐

7. Have you always shopped there   Yes/No

8. Do you know, or are you known, by the shop assistants?   Yes/No

9. Do you consider shopping to be a tedious necessity or do you gain enjoyment from it?   Yes/No/Don't know

10. When you go shopping, which of the following attitudes is foremost in your mind?
    (a) It's got to be done   ....
    (b) I might meet Mrs. So-and-so and have a chat   ....
    (c) It will be a pleasant break from housework   ....
    (d) I must look for good value   ....

11. When buying groceries, do you prefer to
    (a) buy a few items at a time?   ....
    (b) buy the whole week's groceries at one time?   ....

12. At the grocers which you patronise, do you also buy meat, fruit and vegetables?   Yes/No

    With particular regard to counter-service and self-service grocers:

13. Do you feel that *you* could steal from a self-service grocers if you so wished?   Yes/No
    Do you think it would be easy to steal?   Yes/No
    If NO, why not?...
    ....

14. Which type of shop do you feel freer and more independent in?
        C/S ☐   S/S ☐

15. Do you associate either type of shop with a class concept?
        Yes ☐   No ☐

16. Do you feel that you are tempted to buy more in a self-service shop because the goods look more tempting or do you feel that because there is a wide range of choice you can buy the exact amount you can afford?
    ....

17. Do you feel goods are likely to be fresher in a self-service shop, due possibly to higher turnover?   Yes/No

18. Do you think branded goods are cheaper in a self-service shop, and thus you get more value for money?   Yes/No

19. Do you consider that the self-service shop stocks a wider variety of goods than the ordinary grocer?   Yes/No

20. Do you regard the counter-service grocery shop as a traditional form which has given good service for a long time?   Yes/No

21. Do you think of the self-service shop as something large and impersonal and not really requiring the loyalty that would be afforded to a small grocer who you know?   Yes/No

22. Do you agree with the following statements?
    (a)   Self-service shops are cheap, efficient and clean   Yes/No
    (b)   Self-service shops are expensive, inefficient and unhygienic   Yes/No
    (c)   Counter-service shops are friendly, warm and personal   Yes/No
    (d)   Assistants in counter-service shops are always more helpful and efficient than in self-service shops   Yes/No
    (e)   You can pop into a counter-service shop for occasional items, but you have to buy in larger quantities in a self-service shop.   Yes/No

23. Do you go out to work?   Yes/No

24. Do you have a car?   Yes/No

25. What social class would you say you were?
    Working ☐   Lower-middle ☐   Middle ☐   Upper-middle ☐

Comments on the Shopping Schedule

A general point to begin: the first three questions are what we call classification data, necessary for analysis of respondents' social characteristics but not obviously relevant to them so far as the object of the survey is concerned. These questions are best left till last when they can be used as 'finishing off questions' when respondents have got used to answering questions. For women particularly it is not at all good tactics to ask a woman her age in the very first question. Actually, in interviews, women nowadays very rarely raise any difficulties over this question, but it is certainly best left until a little 'rapport' has been established.

Q. 1. The wording 'What is your Age?' is very formal. An interviewer would more naturally ask 'Do you mind if I ask how old you are?' This could be put on the schedule as simply 'How old are you?' and the interviewer can add a suitable preparatory phrase. The response categories are faulty since they overlap. A person aged 30, 40, 50 or 60 exactly could be ticked in two boxes. To make these age ranges suitable for analysis purposes they should be 20–29, 30–39, and so on.

Q. 2. A person actually asked 'What is your marital status?' might well be baffled as to what this meant, and could even be very insulted. 'Marital status' is a technical term. Far better to ask 'Are you single, or married or widowed?' The question of divorced people can be tricky and if they *must* be used for analysis purposes it is best to ask the question quite openly; otherwise they can be included as whatever category is most appropriate—usually it is 'widowed or divorced'.

Note also that the order of the boxes would be more logical if they went Single, Married, Widowed, which is a natural progression, rather than hopping back from Married to Single.

Q. 3. 'Dependent children' may well baffle many people, so the question needs to be phrased so that children are sorted out into the categories needed for analysis purposes. For this survey probably categories of 'pre-school', 'at school, living at home' and any other categories such as 'education, away from home' or 'working, living at home' would be meaningful. These then would need to be categorised for the response so that a table on the schedule would seem useful. It would also be better to instruct the interviewers that this question should be asked only of married or widowed women. There may be single women with dependent children, but it is best for this to come out later in the interview, as it surely will. The direct confrontation of ordinary spinsters with this question would lose goodwill.

Q. 4. A question of this type can be a useful starter to an interview so long as it does not necessitate complicated calculations. The problem with the actual question as it is here phrased is that 'this district' is too vague. People move around within towns and cities and subjective ideas of districts vary. Probably 'this house' would be better.

Q. 5. This question rather pre-supposes that people (a) stick to one shop, (b) do have a 'main' grocer.

A re-phrasing to take into account these points would probably use some specific items of regular purchases (such as fats) and would ask where these are normally bought. But buying patterns (especially when groceries are delivered, or where people call at super-markets on their way home) can vary enormously and probably more than one question would have to be asked so as to establish various types of shoppers for analysis purposes. These types could probably be ascertained in a pilot survey and could then be used as pre-set answers for the interviewer to check. Probably a class of 'Other, specify . . .' would be needed for people with very individual habits. The main point here is *not* to collect everybody's individual little differences, but to try to work out a limited number of useful categories of shoppers—useful, that is, for analysis purposes. This question, therefore, really needs complete re-thinking, since a respondent who *does* have the one grocer from whom she buys all her groceries will reply by saying what the name and address of the shop is, and these facts are not really going to be analysed.

Q. 6. If the problems of Q. 5 can be solved, then this question seeks to find out whether the 'regular' grocer is a self-service or counter-service type. For reliable answers to this the respondent needs to be given a little explanation so that there is no doubt whatsoever as to what the two terms mean. Note also that the response boxes here are in reverse order to the way in which the question is put. If counter-service precedes self-service in the question it is better to have that order for the response.

Q. 7. The word 'always' is absolutely meaningless. The interviewer wants some idea of how long the informant has shopped there, so a question on these lines must be framed, with appropriate response categories in mind. A problem that could make diffi-culties here is that the shop itself may be a new one, or it might, in recent years, have changed over from counter- to self-service.

Q. 8. The word 'know' can be interpreted in a multitude of ways.

L

Also this is a double question. The respondent may well believe she 'knows' the assistants, but they may not 'know' her. More specific, objective terms are needed.

Q. 9. The wording for the two alternatives is rather extreme, especially 'tedious necessity', and it does not give a happy choice anyway. Shopping is obviously a 'necessity' but people still gain enjoyment from necessities. The major error, however, lies in the response categories, since a 'yes' or a 'no' is absolutely meaningless as a reply to the question put.

Q. 10. This is an example of a question which is put to the respondent with a selection of answers actually suggested. The respondent can be given two alternatives; either she indicates *all* the answers with which she agrees, or else she must choose only one which is paramount. This question asks for one answer (*foremost* in her mind) but gives a choice which is not conducive to picking out one. A housewife could answer 'yes' to all four of the suggestions but she would have great difficulty in deciding if any one suggestion could be said to be 'foremost in her mind' since the four ideas are of different kinds, not a series of gradations of one idea.

Q. 11. This is mainly at fault for giving only two extreme choices and leaving out an obvious middle one of the women who buys more than just a few items more than once a week.

Q. 12. An example of a triple question. Only a 'yes' or a 'no' is recorded whereas three yes/no categories are needed for the meat, the fruit and the vegetables.

Q. 13. This was a genuinely suggested question based on the fact that pilfering is high in many self-service shops. It would, however, be very unfortunate to place such a blunt question as this before most honest housewives and both embarrassment and anger could be the result.

Q. 14 This question demonstrates an instance where the question asker obviously has an idea that could be interesting but has not thought about the question answerer. To be free and independent in a grocery shop is a very vague idea which could very easily baffle many a below average intelligence respondent.

Q. 15. A beautiful example of sociological jargon. The very wording is reminiscent of some of the worst of sociological writing.

Q. 16. I suggested to my students that this question could well have a pre-coded response category of 'Eh?' One sees what the questioner had in mind, but put in these actual words the result could be hilarious.

Q. 17. This would be all right as one question about fresher goods in self-service shops, but the addition of one possible reason complicates the whole issue and makes a response impossible in simple yes/no terms.

Q. 18. This is the same problem as Q.17, of asking a question and then requiring a particular reason to be accepted with it.

Q. 19. This, like questions 17 and 18, is a leading question which expects the answer 'yes', unless the respondent is prepared to make a special effort of denying the positive suggestion put. Questions 17 and 18 were rather obscured by being difficult in other ways, but all three questions are very clearly biased towards the self-service shop.

Q. 20. This question is biased the other way, towards the counter-service shop, and manages to be double as well. It also contains a description of the counter-service as being 'a traditional form' which is not a very clear concept anyway.

Q. 21. Another example of a long involved question which is leading and double at the same time. The phraseology of 'loyalty that would be afforded' is somewhat theoretical and not all counter-service grocers are small.

Q. 22. This clearly should lead off with a choice between agreeing or disagreeing with statements which follow; as it stands the respondent is almost challenged to disagree if he has the courage. The questions (a), (b) and (c) are triple ones since, for example, a shop can be clean but not cheap or efficient, and so on. Question (d) is double; probably many of us know helpful assistants who are not efficient. Also the extreme word 'always' would probably be too dogmatic for most people. Question (e) is difficult to understand, and the words 'occasional items' are most obscure. The idea is there but re-phrasing is needed.

Q. 23. Before moving from the questions about shopping to questions of a personal sort, a line of instructions to interviewers would be wise, with a suggested linking phrase such as 'I am now going to leave shopping and I want to ask a few questions about you yourself'. Question 23 itself is very simple in wording, but a reply of 'yes' could mean so many different things that it is unlikely to be adequate. The point of importance in this survey is that a housewife who does go out to work at all could have patterns of shopping which might be strongly affected by the hours she works, the place where she works, how she gets to work and so on. A simple yes/no to this question is likely to be grossly inadequate for analysis purposes and suggests that the survey designer has not thought much about analysis.

Q. 24. This is another rather bald question which suggests a number of further necessary questions. The word 'you' could be interpreted as either the respondent herself or her husband and herself, with gross errors in responses. Many middle class housewives have their own personal cars, many more have regular use of their husband's car for shopping.

Q. 25. This question, as set out here, is a rather frontal attack on a somewhat emotional topic. If an *objective* measure of social status is to be used for analysis the husband's occupation is normally used as the index. If *subjective* social class is to be used, by a respondent's self-rating, then some objective criteria are normally required for check purposes. As this question stands it is in a somewhat crude form and there is no indication to interviewers as to whether the four categories are to be suggested to informants or whether the informant gives an unprompted answer and the interviewer ticks the nearest box which he himself considers most appropriate. Where a prompt is to be given it is usual for the interview schedule to have the word PROMPT clearly displayed.

General Remarks

It is not possible in an introductory textbook of this length to deal with every type of problem which arises from framing questions for interview schedules or questionnaires. The reader can best develop his expertise by examining critically as many schedules and questionnaires as he can find and by gathering together his own personal collection. These should include not only serious ones used in research projects but also less serious ones as sometimes put forward in news-papers and magazines. It is becoming much more common today for books which give the results of sample surveys to include a copy of the questionnaire or schedule in an appendix. If this is not done it is by no means a bad idea to write to the author asking for a copy for one's self. (When doing this it should be remembered that a self-addressed envelope with stamp may well produce a better response.) Unfortunately it is rarely feasible for journals to reproduce question-naires or schedules but authors of research papers are nearly always pleased to have people take an interest in their work and a request for a questionnaire is unlikely to be refused. But, once again, whilst a critical approach to other people's work is desirable, it is equally important to be able to work constructively oneself. So whenever one finds a poor question the real benefit will come not merely from spotting the error but from going on from there and producing an improved version of it.

A Note on Guided Questionnaires

This section is included here rather than with the section on question-naires since it is concerned primarily with matters of detail in helping people to answer questions. Most of the examples used in this book have dealt with interview schedules used for individual interviews or questionnaires sent through the post. But particular circumstances either necessitate, or may even give the opportunity for, particular techniques of enquiry. I have myself reported on some of the very interesting problems which arose in surveying a theatre audience.[1] Another situation where questionnaires were used in somewhat novel circumstances was in a pilot survey, never published, of church congregations which I carried out. In this survey the congregations of several churches were given questionnaires during a service, mainly asking for very simple details of sex, marital status, residence, occupation and education. To save space and to reduce the amount of wording on the questionnaires themselves the operation was carried out with the vicar taking all the respondents through the questions with comments on each of them read out by him from a prepared

[1] See *British Journal of Sociology*, Vol. XVII, No. 4, December 1966.

guide. In this way something between an interview and a questionnaire was used and the project had the advantage of verbal explanations to the questions with respondents recording their own responses. Where the groups to be studied can be gathered together, as in a church or theatre, and in such institutions as schools and colleges, the problems of question asking can be reduced by being prepared to experiment with variations on established methods.

Measurement of Attitudes

The whole question of attitudes, scaling and measurement of opinions is far too great and involved to be dealt with in any detail in this book. Fortunately there has recently been published a book[2] which does give the reader a clear explanation of the major problems involved in this special aspect of survey methodology, and most general text books in social psychology have a section on this work.

An attitude is essentially a mental disposition towards some potential action. Whilst actions can be observed attitudes can only be inferred. But it is obvious that attitudes are vitally important to social scientists who wish to find out how people feel about potential situations. A general election is always preceded by a great increase in opinion polling in which people are asked how they intend to vote within the next few weeks, but polls are being taken between elections at regular intervals in which people may be asked 'If there were an election next week, how would you vote?' This latter approach is getting away from the actual and more towards the potential. Attitudes are often characterised, for questioning, by sentences beginning with 'if'.

It is useful to consider attitude studies according to the scales devised by a number of social scientists. In passing, it is of interest to note that all of them are Americans, an indication of the lead given in this work by that country. Five types of attitude studies may be instanced.

The Bogardus Social Distance Scale

This scale was developed in the 1920s in an attempt to measure the

[2] See A. N. Oppenheim: *Questionnaire Design and Attitude Measurement*, London, 1966.

intensity of national/racial feelings. The respondent is asked to say within what 'social distance' he would be willing to allow certain nationalities or races to approach. The steps used, in descending degree of closeness are:

1. Close relations by marriage.
2. Personal friends in your club.
3. Neighbours in your street.
4. Colleagues at work.
5. Citizens of your country.
6. Tourists in your country.
7. Forbidden to reside in your country.

A scale such as this is relatively easy to handle and score and may be used for simple comparisons between races and nationalities. But it is difficult to know whether 'social distance' as a concept is really measured by such a scale; in the U.S.A. people put the French at a further distance than the English, yet in other questions expressed greater sympathy towards the French. It is also difficult to establish 'steps' in the scale which are accepted as quite discrete and of reasonably equal distance. For instance, in the scale above 'forbidden to reside', it could be argued, should be item 6 since 'residing' is more permanent than being a tourist; otherwise item 7 should have 'reside' replaced by 'enter'.

With all its problems the social distance scale is a helpful approach and has been the basis for many attempts at measurement, one interesting one being developed during the 1939–45 war by Crespi to measure social rejection of conscientious objectors.

The Thurstone Scale

This form of scaling, devloped in the late 1920s, uses a method whereby the respondent is asked to agree or disagree with given statements. The formulation of the scale begins by the investigators collecting together a large number of statements, perhaps several hundred, with which so far as is possible respondents can clearly agree or disagree. A panel of experts on the topic for study is then got together (they can be any number, even up to a hundred) and they are asked to classify the statements in a given range, say 7, 9 or

11 columns, ranging from the most favourable right across to the most unfavourable, with a mid-point of neutrality (which is why an odd number of columns is used). The investigators are looking for those statements which the experts generally agree should go into one column, or within a narrow range; statements which the experts 'spread' between columns are thrown out. The statements gaining most agreement then go into the column which is closest to their 'average' placing. In this way the original large number of statements is greatly reduced by rejecting the ambiguous and the ones securing little agreement, and after further sifting by the investigators usually something between fifteen and thirty statements are kept and these are chosen to give equal distances (by the median place of each question) and thus when put together form a continuum from one extreme of attitudes to the other.

When a respondent does the exercise the statements are shuffled to randomise them and the subject picks out those statements with which he agrees. His attitude is then measured by the median values of his selected agreement statements.

Whilst this scale has its attractions for measuring purposes it can be seen that the need for a panel of experts to do the original scrutiny raises problems. A simpler system is the following one.

The Lickert Scale

Developed in the early 1930s this is a scale which can only be used for a relative appraisal between respondents in a group. The Thurstone scale, having been standardised by the experts, can be used on any individual since the limits have already been set. The Lickert scale does away with the experts and uses the rest of a group for the comparison. The investigators begin, rather like the Thurstone process, by collecting a large number of statements, but in this exercise the relevance of the statements is not terribly important and there is no panel of experts to scrutinise them. The subjects are given the statements and usually are asked to indicate complete approval, approval, neutrality, disapproval or complete disapproval on a five points scale. Each respondent's total mark is got by adding up choices for every question. The scores obtained by each proposition are then correlated with the total marks and statements with low correlations are discarded. This method of testing by 'internal consistency' means that each individual can only be seen relative to the group of respondents of which he is a part, and a Lickert scale must therefore be relative as against the absoluteness of the Thurstone scale.

Guttman Scalograms

This technique was developed during the 1939–45 war and is a method which tries to develop a hierarchical scale in which agreement with one statement must mean agreement with preceding statements. The statements used in the Thurstone scale would be of a hierarchical nature—if one was prepared to accept a person of a given nationality as ones brother-in-law this would presume accepting him as a club-member, neighbour, work-mate and so on. The Guttman scale tries to find hierarchies of statements which produce general agreement by respondents on the hierarchy. It can be seen that if agreement with statements does follow a hierarchical pattern and people who respond to them show a general trend then a scale may be constructed from the items agreed on. No matter how far people go in their agreement the point is that they agree in the correct pattern to statements below their own personal limit. To construct a Guttman scale therefore requires a tremendous amount of playing around with the respondents and their responses to try to find which statements are most hierarchical from the respondents' answers.[3] As a rule those statements which gain a 90 per cent agreement on their hierarchical positions from the respondents are included in the scale and others are rejected. To enable the investigators to move answers about special boards have been produced and punched card techniques devised.

Sociometry and Sociograms

This technique, which was devised by the psychologist Moreno in the 1930s, is essentially a way of studying personal relationships

[3] See M. Duverger: *Introduction to the Social Sciences*, London, 1964, pp. 206–7, for an illustration of a Guttman Scale in construction.

between individuals in face-to-face groups. It is therefore very marginal to sociological methods, but it is useful to know of it since small-group sociology is now becoming a more important part of sociological investigation. Basically the sociogram is a diagrammatic representation of feelings of attraction or rejection between people in a group. For example, men in a work group may be asked who they would most like to work with, and perhaps who they would least like to work with. Answers can be limited to one choice, or extended to multiple choices, though any great extension makes the sociograms difficult to reproduce. From the replies the individuals can be depicted on paper by numbers or letters and joined together by lines of attraction and differing style lines of rejection. A completed sociogram will show who are the most chosen 'stars' of a group and who are the isolates. It will also show patterns of cliques, pairs and chains of relationships. Good leadership (as in military groups such as aircrews) will give stars and general attraction to the leaders; poor leadership will give pairs and cliques and rejection of the leaders. By giving simple scores to amounts of attraction and repulsion expressed individuals can be scored for choice or rejection status, and group cohesion can be scored by the amount of mutual pairs and other attraction patterns.

In General about Attitudes and Measurement

The above brief signposts to established ways of measuring attitudes are given here to let the beginning surveyor know that, especially in psychology and social psychology, a great deal of work on measurement has been done already. If one is interested in trying to gain some measurement of attitudes to coloured people, religion, war and so on, it is worth while asking the psychologists if they can advise on any standardised scales for measurement. It may be that a scale exists and can be used in a survey, with the valuable bonus of comparative material already being available. It may be that a scale is too long or too complicated to be incorporated in a sociological interview or questionnaire (psychologists so often get people into their laboratories for thirty minute tests) but to ignore the possibilities of using well constructed tests is foolish.

9

Analysis and Presentation of Results

Introduction

In previous pages about the various ways in which questions can be asked, it has been stressed throughout that questions are themselves only stimuli and it is the responses that matter. Every survey enquiry ends up with a number of completed interview schedules or questionnaires. The number of them may be under a hundred in the case of an undergraduate dissertation (or even a more advanced study of respondents in depth) or it may result in several thousands of replies. In my own six weeks survey of a theatre audience the complete response was near to 12,000 questionnaires and storage alone was a problem, even before analysis began.

It is, therefore, vitally important to consider *as early as possible* in a survey how material is going to be analysed and presented. If the study stems, as it should do in sociological enquiry, from the wish to test a hypothesis, or to refine a theory or a concept, then there is a pattern which is determined by the problem itself. As was said very early in this book, not every sociological enquiry entails a social survey. Many sociological enquiries use documentary sources, often of a historical type. These studies may eventually lead to empirical field enquiries, but in many cases they do not and they are none the worse for it. Indeed it is highly desirable for researchers to recognise that a field survey is only to be undertaken if the nature of the enquiry necessitates information being gained through this method. Surveys are hard work, time consuming and often expensive; there is no sense in dashing into them simply because everyone seems to be doing a survey these days.

If this warning is kept in mind then many surveys can be avoided altogether and alternative, perhaps better, sources of data can be used. Where surveys *do* appear to be necessary they will show themselves to be necessary because of the *answers* that are needed. From the required answers the questions will stem, and from the likely answers the analysis can begin. This is not to suggest that a survey designer is going to expect completely cut and dried answers to every question put, but it does mean that if a question is put with no idea at all as to what the likely answers are to be then it is highly likely that the designer does not really know why the question is being asked—apart from the old danger of its being 'interesting'. We should work with the basic presumption that questions are only included in a survey when the question designer has already some fair idea of what answers are likely to come back and what general outline of analysis will be imposed on them.

Pre-Coding of Questions

As an initial step towards classification of likely and useful answers the surveyor can begin by asking himself how he will use the answers received to a question. Let us take a simple case to begin with, that of sex. There is no problem here of deciding what response categories to use, since all respondents will be male or female. In a schedule or questionnaire boxes labelled 'Male' and 'Female' can be included without fear of them being inadequate and the surveyor can go on to think of the ways in which analysis of other factors according to sex may be used to test hypotheses or set down necessary basic information. A series of questions on what people in a family do in their leisure time will obviously need to discriminate between members of the families surveyed and so sex, marital status and age will be necessary variables for analysing other activities. Marital status will normally be dealt with by boxes labelled 'Single', 'Married', 'Widowed or Divorced', and these categories should be sufficiently discriminating unless it is deemed necessary to separate widowed from divorced, or even to include a special category for 'separated' if the survey is looking particularly at problems of family breakdown. The purpose of the enquiry will always dictate the particular analysis categories to be used. When we come to age here we have a continuous rather than a discrete variable and the analysis categories to be used could be of any size at all. The decision as to whether to use, say, a five-year or a ten-year age category can only be decided on the basis of what ideas are being tested. If there is any doubt it is probably best to leave pre-set categories aside and simply use an open box or line on which the interviewer or respondent enters the actual age in years. Coding of this answer can then be done afterwards at the analysis stage.

The point is, then, that by giving a respondent a set of answers to check on a questionnaire, or by giving a set of responses for an interviewer to ring or underline on a schedule one can save writing in of answers and thus avoid the ambiguities (or even illegible hand-writing) which make subsequent analysis difficult. The situation is more important in a self-completed questionnaire than an interview since interviewers can be instructed as to what answers to expect and how to enter them on the schedule, but the person filling in a questionnaire cannot be made to read a whole sheet of instructions and so as many 'hidden' instructions as possible should be incorporated in the questions themselves by means of pre-set response categories. Thus it may be important to get a very detailed analysis of the respondents' type of education and this is by no means an easy question to ask or to get answered clearly. In the theatre survey twelve response categories were given on the questionnaire and the respondent was asked to tick in the box opposite the appropriate one. The twelfth category was an open one for people who did not fit into any of the other eleven. These twelve responses then gave a large number of categories which could be used for analysis and where necessary they could be combined for broader analysis. The following is an actual reproduction of this question:

Please tick in the box opposite the type of school or college you **last attended** full-time or which you **now attend** full-time.

(1) Primary (or elementary) School	☐	(7) Independent Day School	☐
(2) Preparatory School	☐	(8) Independent Boarding School	☐
(3) Secondary Modern School	☐	(9) Technical or Art College	☐
(4) Secondary Technical School	☐	(10) Teacher Training College	☐
(5) Grammar School	☐	(11) University or C.A.T.	☐
(6) Comprehensive School	☐	(12) Other, please say what	☐

....

The usefulness of this sort of pre-set response is that the twelve categories themselves form the basis for any subsequent analyses and the distribution of responses in this survey could be analysed according to sex, age, seats occupied or any other variable believed to be of value. Another example from this survey is the question asking people how they first learned about the play they were watching. Here a pilot survey had indicated the most likely sources and these were printed on the questionnaire so as to help respondents choose, as far as was possible, their own particular sources. To have asked respondents to write in their own answers would probably have resulted in far too many unanalysable responses such as 'an advertisement' or 'I heard about it'. The pre-set answer, we hoped, would overcome these ambiguous or vague replies.

How did you first learn that this play was being produced at the Playhouse?

(1) Newspaper advertisement ☐   (5) Indoor notice   ☐
(2) Outdoor posters   ☐   (6) From a friend   ☐
(3) Playhouse mailing list   ☐   (7) From a relative   ☐
(4) Programme notes   ☐   (8) Don't know   ☐
     (9) Other means, please say how...

The above set of answers meant that in analysing the replies nine predetermined categories would be used and it can be seen that statistical tables could easily be constructed to test hypotheses about where people first learned of this play. For instance, suppose we hypothesized that older people heard about the play more by personal recommendation, whilst younger people learned about it more through formal advertising, then we could easily construct a table to give the details. The decision as to what comprised 'old' and 'young' would be arbitrary, but let us say we decided to analyse the situation by ten-year age groups and then combine them later if we wanted. A table for this might then be as shown on p. 167.

This sort of table is likely to be the end product of a survey, and it is from the distribution of answers to questions put out in such tables that the conclusions on hypotheses will be made. Tables of this type make it clear to all readers on what grounds the writer is making his conclusions. Statements such as 'the bulk of young people learned about the play from formal advertisements' are then referable back to the original data which show clearly what these things mean in numerical terms.

How learned about the play	Ages of respondents					
	To 24	25–34	35–44	45–54	55–64	65 and over
Newspaper advertisement						
Outdoor posters						
Playhouse mailing list						
Programme notes						
Indoor notice						
From a friend						
From a relative						
Don't know						
Other means						
Total						

In analysing survey data in this way analysis decisions must be made quite early on in the planning of the survey if the work is not to be a dreadful task of trying to bring order to a chaos of answers. In the case of the theatre survey, good attendances at two plays along with a high response rate could have resulted in as many as 18,000 questionnaires needing to be analysed. In fact attendance at the plays was not terribly high although the response rate amongst those present was very high indeed, averaging 92 per cent over the six weeks of survey. For analysis on this scale it would have been utterly ludicrous to think of a clerical assistant going through each questionnaire by hand and entering answers onto tally sheets. This process of working directly from the schedules or questionnaires may be feasible with numbers up to about a hundred, but beyond that the task becomes burdensome.

The answer to this problem lies in using mechanical means of analysis whereby a machine rather than a clerk runs through the response categories counting the numbers of responses in the various categories. But, as yet, no machine can read data as well as the human brain does, and so the answers must be translated into very simple language indeed for the machines. This factor of simplification is basic to all understanding of the powers of analysis machines. Even computers are *basically* very simple machines in the actual data they use; their value lies in the incredibly fast speed at which they work and thus the tremendous amount of work they can do in a very short time. But even computers must be programmed, they cannot read information which has not been translated for them into their own very simple language.

Not many social surveys require the use of a computer unless they are going to use a tremendous amount of data or are going to work out great sets of multiple variables for significance tests. A good example of computerised social research is Moser and Scott's study of British towns in which sixty factors of a quantitative type (mainly drawn from Registrar-General's sources) were drawn from 157 towns and cities and the whole was fed into a computer to find out what factors tended to go along with others. From this study a most useful typology of towns was produced which was based on identifiable data, not just descriptive 'feelings'. But this research was unusual. What is much more commonplace in survey work at university or administrative levels is the need for a quick analysis of a few hundred schedules or questionnaires and for this the conventional punched card analysis is adequate.

Punched Card Analysis

As has been said, machines can only do what man arranges for them to do. In the case of the punched card the basic process is to change answers to questions into holes on a specially prepared card so that a machine can 'read' where a hole has been punched and register this fact on a 'counter' for any number of cards. Let us look at the basic process of turning answers to questions into statistical tables by means of punched cards in a practical example. In the theatre survey it was important to analyse a number of questions according to the age of the respondents. They were therefore asked the following question —their replies to be given by ticking in the appropriate box.

In which age group are you?

Do not write in this column

(1) Under 11 ☐   (4) 19–24 ☐   (7) 45–54 ☐
(2) 11–14 ☐   (5) 25–34 ☐   (8) 55–64 ☐   28
(3) 15–18 ☐   (6) 35–44 ☐   (9) 65 or over ☐

The response categories, which are numbered 1 to 9, cover all possible replies and a tick in the box is sufficient to get an answer. It will be noted that each age-group is numbered, and these numbers were, in fact, the code numbers. That is to say that the age group '25–34' when expressed in numerical code becomes 'Code 5', the age group '55–64' becomes 'Code 8', and so on from codes 1 to 9 for this question of age. For the person, whom we will call the 'coder', who is translating answers into punched card language the range of ages has now been translated into a simple series of numbers from 1 to 9, and the appropriate code number in this survey is entered alongside the number 28 in the column headed (to the respondent) 'Do not write in this column'. Let us suppose that the particular respondent is aged 37 and thus falls in the response category '35–44'; he is therefore 'Code 6'.

The conventional punched card used in Britain is now known as an I.C.L. card, these being the initials of the firm of International Computers Limited who have succeeded the pair of firms formerly known as Hollerith and Powers-Samas. An I.C.L. card may come in a variety of sizes, but the standard size has 80 'columns' on it, which means that it can deal with 80 quite separate sets of information. It is easiest to think of this as 80 separate questions which can all have a 'column' each. Each column can be punched in 12 different places, and this actually means that a hole is knocked out of the card at one of 12 pre-determined places on the column. So we may say that for 80 questions we can have up to 12 different answers for each question.

To return to our example of the age categories; in this survey age was the 28th question to be analysed and 9 of the possible responses were used in the 28th column of the card. Thus our respondent aged

M

thirty-seven would be translated, for this question, to look like this:

Column 28

1
2
3
4
5
6̄ (An actual rectangle would be punched out of the card to
7 indicate code 6)
8
9
10
11
12

A facsimile of a proper I.C.L. card is given opposite and it will be seen that the top right hand corner has a small piece cut off; this is to indicate which is front and back since a machine could just as well take in a card back to front if this were not guarded against. The card then has the columns 1 to 80 marked in small numbers and under each column there are small numbers to indicate the codes. Here a rather confusing item must be noted. The actual numbers 1–9 are the last of the 12, and the three top codes of each column come before code 1. The reason for this is a practical one—the cards go through the machines with the top edge leading and it is best to use the first three codes only if necessary as they can weaken the card a little and result in it bending more than is desirable. So the real numbers begin on the fourth possible hole with 1 and continue down to the last possible hole with 9. Then the top 3 holes are regarded rather as reserves to be used if absolutely necessary. Confusion can arise over the codes given to these three holes. In some codes they are labelled Y, X, O., in others V, X, O., and others 11, 10, 0. There seems no sense in this variety of symbols and one single one would be desirable. My own usage is normally Y, X and O for the first three codes but this is purely because these were the ones used on the first survey I was instructed on by a statistician.

An 80-column I.C.T. (now I.C.L.) card slightly reduced from the original size.

The process of punching the appropriate holes in the cards is a rapid one, and is done on a machine simply called a 'punch'. The card is placed on a smooth platen and punching begins on column one, the card moving automatically to the next column after each hole is made. The twelve punch keys are in four rows of three and there is a further key which passes over a column if it is to be left blank. Hand punches are very simple to use and a reasonable expertise can be gained with an hour's practice. For very large numbers of cards it is more economical to have cards punched professionally since the trained punch operators work at very high speeds and, in most punched card bureaux they use console, electrically operated machines which feed in blank cards automatically and remove the punched cards after each operation. The amateur who hires a hand punch for a large number of cards may well be wasting a great deal of time and money.

In reading the code numbers from schedules, questionnaires or specially prepared code sheets the punch operator is always in danger of either misreading a number or hitting the wrong key. To check on punching errors a machine called a 'verifier' is used. All verifiers, even the portable ones, are electrically powered and they work exactly like a punch except that the key does not actually *punch* a hole in the card. If the hole is already cut (i.e. correctly punched) then the verifier 'feeler' makes contact through it and allows the machine to go on to the next column. If the hole is not cut, or is in the wrong place, then the feeler does not go through, but is stopped by the thickness of the card. In this case the machine 'jams' and the operation cannot go on to the next column. The card is then taken out and can be visually examined to see what has been done wrong on this particular column. If there is an error the card must be destroyed and a new one punched. There are few things more infuriating than to discover an error near the end of verifying about 60 or 70 columns. To ensure that a punch operator who misreads a number does not repeat the error on verification it is customary for a different person to verify her punching. When all the cards have been punched and verified they are put together in a pile (usually called a 'set') and they are then ready for the process of sorting.

In the general run of social surveys cards are analysed quickly and accurately on a machine called a 'counter-sorter'. Basically this machine is 'set' to analyse a given column by moving an electrically connected 'feeler' to the appropriate column position over a metal drum. The cards are put at one end of the machine in a pile and are mechanically pushed, from the bottom of the pile, onto the revolving drum. As they go over the drum the 'feeler' runs along the column and where the hole has been punched out to indicate the code an electrical contact is made. This completes a circuit which works a conveyor belt on the other side of the roller and as the cards are carried on this belt they drop through into the correct one of twelve boxes which collect together the cards as they are sorted. The counter-sorter, at the same time registers each card as it goes into its box, so that the numbers in each box are shown after each sort. There is also a grand total indicator which tells how many cards in all have been sorted. So the net result is that our cards are electrically sensed, sent to their appropriate boxes, code by code, and counted as they go in. When the final card has gone through all one has to do is to read the numbers from the set of counters, translate codes back into age categories and we know then the age distribution of our group. The speed at which the sorting is done may be slow by comparison with computers, but at 500 cards per minute it is adequate for most surveys. There is also the advantage that the cards are physically separated into their individual boxes, so if we want next to make a special analysis of some other factor by each age category the cards are already divided up for us and they can be run through on another column set by set. In using a counter-sorter the research worker normally reads off the sub-totals for the boxes and enters these onto his blank tables. If he has access to a more sophisticated punched card installation he can have results printed for him on a 'tabulator'. There are numerous other machines which will help the survey worker, but these will not be dealt with here since they are more complicated and require more programming before use. The essential point being made here is that if one understands the basic problems of coding, punching and using a counter-sorter then one has the grasp of essentials adequate for most everyday social surveys. From punched cards to computers is then merely a further step along the same road, but one we shall not take here.

Recapitulation of the Above Procedures

To make sure that the process of analysis is clearly understood, and also so that we may note a few minor points of detail in addition to the main lines, the basic steps are here laid out in the form of a table.

Process	Details
Hypotheses	Derived from theory or concepts
Questionnaire or schedule topics	The main sections of the enquiry which give rise to questions and necessary classification data.
Questions	Detailed aspects of the topics, each question being relevant to the purpose, not merely 'interesting'.
Coding	Answers are turned into numbers. These may be incorporated in pre-set answers or transcribed after answers are recorded.
Punching	Code numbers are translated into appropriate holes in appropriate columns on the punched cards.
Verifying	Punched cards are checked to ensure accuracy of punching.
Sorting	Set of cards goes through the counter-sorter and, for each column, the numbers in each code are recorded on the counters.
Transcription	Numbers on counters are transcribed onto analysis tables. Code numbers become verbal categories again.
Application to hypotheses	Tables of results are carefully read and applied to the appropriate hypotheses. Tests are applied where necessary on the tables.

Some Points on Coding

It will be seen in the preceding table that coding may be done in a number of ways. In the case of the theatre survey most answers were

pre-set and the actual code numbers were included on the questionnaire in three cases—those of where people learned of the play, their
ages and their education. In a large number of other questions (19 in
all) the respondent was given a question the answer to which was
simply 'yes' or 'no'. In all these cases (19 columns) the code for 'yes'
was always 1 and the code for 'no' was always 2. This uniformity of
very simple coding meant that the coders could easily *memorise* this
actual code. In other cases, such as coding the seat occupied, it was
not so easy and for this coding instructions were needed. It is practically impossible for coding to be done without some sort of written
set of instructions to coders, and so for each survey there is usually
compiled what is called the 'coding manual' or 'code book'. I prefer
the latter term and shall use it here.

In the theatre survey the first question asked respondents to say
what seat they were occupying at the performance which they were
attending. The answer was pre-set to a small degree and given as:

1. **What is your seat for this performance?**

Circle ☐   Stalls ☐   Row letter.........   Seat number......... | 3

(The seat number was actually used only for a check of groups and
does not actually form a part of this particular analysis; ignore that
part of the question). Note that the theatre has only a circle and
stalls, so there was no problem of pits, galleries, upper circles or
other seating categories. Rows and seats in the theatre are clearly
labelled and are, of course, on ticket stubs. The column number for
this question was 3 since columns 1 and 2 dealt with the week and the
day of the performance which were stamped on all completed
questionnaires after collection; this is a good example of a question
which it was *not* necessary or sensible to ask of informants. The seats
in both stalls and circle are in three price ranges according to rows,
so six categories were needed for analysis of replies according to type
of seat occupied. Also a category was needed for people who forget
to answer this question or whose answer was incomplete; this gave a
seventh category. So the code book instructions for this question
were as follows.

Column 3. Question 1. Seat for Performance

Code

1	Circle	Rows A to D
2	Circle	Rows E to H
3	Circle	Rows J to L
4	Stalls	Rows A to C
5	Stalls	Rows D to K
6	Stalls	Rows L to O
0	No answer, or insufficient detail.	

The above coding gives a complete coverage for all answers, or lack of answer, and no reply can fit into more than one code. The coder then takes, let us say, the reply Circle Row G Seat 16, refers to the code book and sees that this is code 2 and writes '2' against column 3 in the coding column of that questionnaire.

Coding with Hand Sort

In the theatre survey 37 columns were used and coding was actually done onto the questionnaire itself, so that the punch operator punched from the codes on the questionnaires themselves. This is not always feasible or desirable in many surveys. The theatre survey had the advantage of having all the questions and thus the columns and their codes on one piece of stiff card, so there was no need for the coder or punch operator to turn any pages. This was most useful in saving time for the puncher especially, since high speed punching and turning of pages do not go well together. In cases where it would be too messy to have the coding on the questionnaires or schedules the codes may be entered onto a 'code sheet'. This is simply a single sheet with column numbers from 1 to 80 printed on it and the coder then enters the appropriate code by the side of the printed column number and the punch operator works from the code sheet rather than the original questionnaire or schedule. A code sheet might look like that shown on the next page.

The appropriate codes are then entered by hand against as many columns as are being used. To use code sheets introduces an extra document between questionnaire and punched card, but it may be considered worthwhile in the case of lengthy questionnaires or in particular surveys where the confidentiality of replies is of particular importance. In the latter case the coders would be specially chosen and after they have transcribed the answers onto code sheets the punchers would not be dealing with any identifiable material.

Survey..................		Questionnaire No....	
I	21	41	61
2	22	42	62
3	23	43	63
4	24	44	64
5	25	45	65
18	38	58	78
19	39	59	79
20	40	60	80

A further point in analysis is worth considering here in so far as smaller surveys are concerned where punched card facilities are not available. If there is to be a lot of cross analysis of information, and turning over several pages of questionnaires or schedules would be very slow and tiring, it is worth considering coding the answers onto code sheets and analysing the code sheets *by hand*. I have done this for a survey of 350 replies on a schedule covering six pages of foolscap and, with a friend or clerk to keep the tally, the person counting through the code sheets can, with a rubber finger stall, get through the code sheets at a fair speed.

Cope Chat Cards

A very simple form of punched card analysis is possible with a method produced by the Cope-Chat company. They use a card, varying in size, with a row of holes along the edges. The surveyor then uses a punch very like a railway ticket collector's punch to cut part of the hole away. These cut-away-holes then indicate the answers to questions. To take a simple example, suppose that holes

1, 2, 3, 4 denoted: 1 = single, 2 = married, 3 = widowed, 4 = divorced. Then to cut out the edge of 2 with the punch would mean

```
 1  2   3   4
┌──────────────────────────
│O ⊔ O   O   O   O
│O
│O
│O
```

that this respondent was married. If all the cards of respondents are then put in a row behind each other in a filing box and a rod is passed through hole 2 it will go through complete holes for codes 1, 3 and 4 but through cut holes for code 2, the married people. This means that codes other than 2 will be 'skewered' by the rod and can be lifted out of the box, but code 2, having a cut-away top will drop down and not be lifted out. These cards can then be counted for analysis. It will be seen that quite complex codes can be obtained by using several holes together. Using four holes, numbered 1, 2, 3 and 4 one can produce extra codes by punching $4+1 = 5$, $4+2 = 6$, $4+3 = 7$, $4+3+1 = 8$ and $4+3+2+ = 9$. For a code up to 9 three skewers would be used. This form of punched card analysis has the undoubted advantage of being cheap in capital equipment since only a few skewers and a punch are needed. Some researchers, especially in universities, are fond of this system though I personally find it too tedious for what it produces. But obviously the manufacturers would disagree and the reader should be aware of this system and prepared to consider it if it seems appropriate for the work to be done.

Presentation of Results

Some people, especially undergraduates working on their first survey, worry about whether they are asking their informants for enough information. These people usually finish up at the analysis stage wondering what to do with the masses information they have collected. It cannot be stressed too much or too often that no information should be collected simply for the sake of information collecting. The factor of relevance becomes very clearly apparent at the stage when the research report is to be written up. So often a thesis or dissertation contains a very large appendix of 'supplementary tables' and the experienced eye quickly sees that what this really means is that 'I collected all this information and I really don't know what to do with it since it really isn't relevant to the point of my thesis, so I'll stick it in an appendix rather than throw it away and perhaps it will impress my examiner.'

Tables of results are compiled to make a point, not to make padding. If they have a job to do and a valid reason for existing they are likely to find a place in the text rather than in an appendix. This is not to say that appendices are all just rubbish dumps—this would be quite misleading—but there is a difference between an appendix which contains a highly detailed discussion on sampling, or a special form of significance testing which would hold up the flow of the main argument and the appendix which simply contains all those tables which were left over when the narrative had been written.

Presenting Results

Let us, therefore, look at the form which a research report may take. Opinions differ widely about points of detail in presenting research findings so what follows must be a personal view. It seems to me that in all writing, from a first year undergraduate essay through to Ph.D. thesis there is a similar pattern for presentation. This can be put very briefly indeed in three stages:

(1) Say what you intend to write about.
(2) Write about it.
(3) Come to a conclusion.

If we take it that (1) is the introduction in which the problem is briefly but clearly stated and that (3) is the drawing together of the threads, which should not be a complete re-statement of all that has already been said, then neither (1) nor (3) need be very long. This leaves (2) as the main part of the writing, and from a sociological point of view it can be sub-divided into a number of sections. I have made it clear in earlier pages that I consider a *sociological* study, as opposed to a merely *social* one, stems from some theoretical or conceptual starting point. If this is so then it is important that the writer makes plain what the starting point is. This then is what we will call the theoretical introduction, and since it comes from theory then it is necessary to explain clearly what the theory is and what work has already been done in this field. From this general consideration the writer may then go on to a more detailed consideration of the particular piece of work which he is about to attempt. This means that he will be looking in much greater detail at a more closely limited field of study and he will go into more detail in theory and will introduce other people's researches where appropriate. From this stage he will then be able to develop his own hypotheses and the reader follows through his own particular line of thought and appreciates what is to be done and why. At this stage the writer will develop his own empirical ideas and the actual enquiry to be carried out will be outlined, with the relevance of the enquiry never in doubt. Whether the enquiry is to include a sample survey or whether it never goes outside the library does not really matter, since the writer will be presenting data which he has collected to test the thesis he is putting forward. The next stage is the description of the means used to collect the data and this will lead on to the presentation of the data themselves, organised in a form appropriate to the needs of the study. If these results are clearly presented, always being used to illustrate and illuminate the points of the hypotheses then they will tell their own story and the conclusions need only be relatively brief.

It will be seen that this programme suggests the desirability of a 'flow' which comes from one section leading naturally into the next. If the research is properly thought out and planned the naturalness *will* be there. If the research has been badly planned and not adequately thought out in advance then the natural flow will be replaced by a jerky progression which will show where the parts fail to fit together properly. The research which is good to read, clearly presented and satisfying in its results does not just happen out of the blue —the ten per cent inspiration must be built around and supported by the ninety per cent perspiration.

It will be seen that the above outline also helps the researcher to clarify the relationship between his own research and that of the general field within which he is working. Since any one research project can only contribute a very little to the advancement of sociological knowledge it is important for beginners especially to recognise the need for scaling down their enquiries to a size which will result in useful special contributions rather than trying to rewrite, let us say, the whole of industrial sociology in one three-year project. Sociologists are very often, by the very nature of their interests, 'big' in their thinking. No one would want sociology to become suffocated in detail; but complex structures (such as bodies of theory) are made up from well constructed small parts, and the major developments in the natural sciences have come from an understanding of minutely small things such as chromosomes and particles.

Suggestions for Further Reading

This book is intended only as a starter in the field of sociological investigation. Although some signposts to further lines of study may have been given in the various chapters, it may be useful to end with a section devoted entirely to suggestions about what may be useful in further reading. It is not difficult to collect together long lists of publications in book form and in journals which, strung together, give a solid impression of scholarship. Unfortunately one result of this process is to bewilder the student, who cannot sort out the elementary from the advanced, the general from the specific and the easy-to-read from the difficult. What follows are a few topic headings under which I have grouped a number of references which I think a student either *should* read because they are important or might well read because they are useful and enlightening. I have not distinguished between these two forms, since some important books are a frightful bore to wade through, worthy though they may be. The list is therefore a personal one; I know I have left out some books which may be more favoured by some sociologists. No personal list can please everyone.

General Books on Methodology, often with a leaning to Theory

C. Wright Mills: *The Sociological Imagination*. Oxford University Press, London and New York, 1959.
Everyone should read this book simply for the joy of it. Mills writes to provoke those who measure everything and understand nothing, and his plea for a historical perspective in sociology is most valuable.

Barbara Wootton: *Testament for Social Science*. Allen & Unwin, London, 1950.

The later chapters are not so relevant, and the book is now dated, but Barbara Wootton is always good value for her forthright arguments. In this book her chapters on scientific investigation are stimulating.

John Madge: *The Development of Scientific Sociology*. Tavistock Publications, London, 1963.

A heavyweight 600 pages, expensive, but for this country perhaps the most useful collection of appraisals of well-known researches seen from a methodological viewpoint. Especially useful for chapters on the Polish Peasant, Kinsey's studies of sexual behaviour and Whyte's Street Corner study.

Q. Gibson: *The Logic of Social Enquiry*. Routledge & Kegan Paul, London; Humanities Press, New York, 1960.

Deals with anti-scientific views about social enquiry and the logical peculiarities of this field. Chapters on facts and values, objectivity, chance, tendency statements.

W. I. B. Beveridge: *The Art of Scientific Investigation*. Heinemann, London; Norton, New York, 1957.

Readable book with many examples of chance findings which have affected scientific discovery. General book to dip into.

Arnold M. Rose: *Theory and Methods in Social Research*. University of Minnesota Press, Minneapolis, 1954.

Essays by author grouped into sections including values in social research, methodological issues in sociology, scientific techniques in sociology.

Gunnar Myrdal: *Value in Social Theory: a Selection of Essays on Methodology*. Routledge & Kegan Paul, London, 1958.

The author of *An American Dilemma*; collected essays include relations between social theory and social policy, valuations and beliefs, the study of the negro problem.

Max Weber: *The Methodology of the Social Sciences*. Translated and edited by Edward Shils and Henry Finch, Free Press, Glencoe, 1949.

Essays written between 1903 and 1917 on 'ethical neutrality' in sociology and economics, 'objectivity' in social science and social policy, critical studies in the logic of the cultural sciences and objective possibility and adequate causation in historical explanation.

Emile Durkheim: *The Rules of Sociological Method*. Translated by
Sarah Solovay and John Muella and edited by George Catlin.
Free Press, Glencoe, 1950.
Chapters on the concept of the 'social fact' and how to observe it,
rules for distinguishing between the normal and the pathological,
how to classify social types, how to explain social facts and how
to establish sociological proofs. Originally published in 1895 and
one of Durkheim's briefest works.

Text Books on More Practical Aspects of Sociological Research

Margaret Stacey: *Methods of Social Research*. Pergamon, Oxford,
1969.
A very clear and well-written introductory text.

Max Adler: *Lectures in Market Research*. Crosby-Lockwood, London,
1965.
Actually presented in lecture note form, and a useful starter for
survey methods in general.

W. J. Goode and P. K. Hatt: *Methods in Social Research*. McGraw-
Hill, New York, 1952.
My personal choice as a basic text book for social research. General
coverage from problems of science to presentation of report.
Available in shiny-back.

John Madge: *The Tools of Social Science*. Longmans, Green & Co.,
London; Doubleday, New York, 1953.
Probably the best all-round British book. Useful sections on language and logic and thoughtful discussion of problems of experiments. Available in shiny-back.

G. Lundberg: *Social Research*. Longmans, Green & Co., New York,
1962.
Very stimulating writing by a no-nonsense scientific approach
man (neo-positivist to his critics). A good all round text.

C. A. Moser: *Survey Methods in Social Investigation*. Heinemann,
London, 1958.
Mainly on surveys, their history and form, with very useful
British examples. Excellent not-too-technical sections on sam-
pling.

T. C. McCormick and R. G. Francis: *Methods of Research in the Behavioural Sciences*. Harper & Bros., New York, 1958.
Reasonably elementary text of 237 pages covering problem choice, research design, documents, measurement, sampling, surveys and presentation.

M. W. Riley: *Sociological Research: a Case Approach*. Harcourt, Brace and World, New York, 1963.
An interesting book which uses various research projects, including Whyte's *Street Corner Society* and Thomas and Znaniecki's *Polish Peasant*, as a basis for discussing various types of research. A big book of over 750 pages, but worth trying.

L. Festinger and D. Katz (eds.): *Research Methods in the Social Sciences*. Dryden Press, New York, 1953.
Readings on sample surveys, field studies, sampling, methods of collecting data, analysis, applications of findings. Not restricted to sociology.

M. Jahoda, M. Deutsch and S. W. Cook: *Research Methods in Social Relations*. Dryden Press, New York, 1951, originally 2 Vols.
Vol. 1 has chapters on selection and formulation of research problems, measurement, collecting data, analysis and presentation, research and theory.
Vol. 2 has readings on questionnaire and schedule construction, interviewing, observation, content analysis, sociometry, panels, sample design, scaling. A very comprehensive work, worth persevering with.

Particularly Concerned with Interviewing and Asking Questions

A. N. Oppenheim: *Questionnaire Design and Attitude Measurement*. Heinemann, London; Basic Books, New York, 1966
General problems of survey and question design and question wording, with chapters on checklists, rating scales and inventories, attitude statements, scaling methods, projective techniques and quantification of data. Good detail and clear presentation.

B. H. Junker: *Field Work: an Introduction to the Social Sciences*. University of Chicago Press, 1960.
Chapters on the meaning of field work, observing, recording and

N

reporting, observational roles, and learning to do field work. Not restricted to sociology. Interesting approach.

R. K. Merton, M. Fiske and P. L. Kendall: *The Focused Interview: a Manual of Problems and Procedures*. Free Press, Glencoe, 1956.

A well known book with a useful 14 page summary at the beginning. Chapters on purposes and criteria, retrospection, range, specificity, depth, personal contexts, group interviews.

S. A. Richardson, B. S. Dobrenwend and D. Klein: *Interviewing: its Forms and Functions*. Basic Books, New York, 1965.

Sections on the interview as a research instrument, respondent participation, the question-answer process, interviewer and respondent.

S. L. Payne: *The Art of Asking Questions*. Princeton University Press, New Jersey, 1951.

Almost exclusively devoted to the wording of single questions, but most entertainingly written.

R. L. Kahn and C. F. Cannell: *The Dynamics of Interviewing*. John Wiley, New York, 1957.

Rather psychologically oriented, sections on techniques for motivating respondents, formulation of objectives, questions and questionnaires, interviews, measurement, probing. Gives selected examples of interviewing in research.

H. H. Hyman, *et al.*: *Interviewing in Social Research*. University of Chicago Press, 1965.

Very detailed study of interviewing, with chapters on interviewer effect, respondent reaction, situational effects and reduction and control of error.

On Documentary Sources

Most general text books have a section on documentary sources, but the following are rather specialised references.

L. Gottschalk, C. Kluckhohn and R. C. Angell: *The Use of Personal Documents in History, Anthropology and Sociology*. Social Sciences Research Council, New York, 1947.

The title indicates the contents clearly enough. Three most useful essays, all of value to the sociologist.

W. I. Thomas and F. Znaniecki: *The Polish Peasant in Europe and America*. Knopf, New York (2 vols.), 1927 (repr. 1958).
A classic study in which letters, newspapers, magazines and a 300 page autobiography are used. Should be looked at in collaboration with the following reference.

H. Blumer: *An Appraisal of 'The Polish Peasant'*. Social Science Research Council, New York, 1939.
A thorough critical appraisal of the methodology, theory and conclusions of the Polish Peasant with discussion of its limitations.

J. Dollard: *Criteria for the Life History*. Peter Smith, Gloucester, Mass., 1949.
Seven rules for using life histories in research applied to six illustrative cases including the autobiography from *The Polish Peasant*.

B. Berelson: *Content Analysis in Communication Research*. Free Press, Glencoe, 1952.
Still the standard work on the analysis of the contents of communication processes. The first 'what' of 'who says what to whom, how and with what effect'. Characteristics, producers, audience, effects, categories.

On Statistical Methods

There are dozens of books on statistics, but many presume more mathematical knowledge than is found in the usual arts background of the would-be sociologist. The following seem to me to be useful for people with little mathematical background or ability.

Darrell Huff: *How to Lie with Statistics*. Gollancz, London; Norton, New York, 1954.
A humorous book with a wealth of wisdom between its covers. Learn the basic principles and enjoy yourself at the same time.

W. J. Reichman: *Use and Abuse of Statistics*. Pelican edition 1964.
An excellent introduction to the purpose of statistics with many apt illustrations. A most useful beginner to understand what statistics are about before getting involved in formulae.

T. G. Connolly and W. Sluckin: *An Introduction to Statistics for the Social Sciences*. Cleaver-Hume, London, 1957 (repr. 1962).
In my opinion *the* simplest introduction to statistical calculations for the uninitiated and mathematically untouched social scientist.

H. E. Garrett: *Statistics in Psychology and Education.* Longmans, London; McKay, New York, 5th edition 1958 (repr. 1965).

Can be used as a more sophisticated version of Connolly and Sluckin as the formulae used are practically identical. The statistics for psychologists and educationists are meaningful to sociologists.

G. Kalton: *Introduction to Statistical Ideas for Social Scientists.* Chapman & Hall, London; Barnes & Noble, New York, 1966.

A very small 58 page monograph giving the absolute essentials of most of the common statistical procedures and tests. Very useful for reference, but too condensed to use as a text. Good value at 6s.

Freda Conway: *Sampling: an Introduction for Social Scientists.* Allen & Unwin, London; Humanities Press, New York, 1967.

Written for the non-mathematical social scientist, and covers clearly the usual range of a text book. But rather expensive at 35s. for 150 pages in hard back edition.

F. R. Oliver: *What do Statistics Show?* Hodder & Stoughton, London, 1964.

A useful introductory text using a literary approach to explain rather more than most books what statistics are *for*. Not a text so much as a general reader.

Some Miscellaneous References

The following books are all of use in one way or another but do not fall easily into a single category. To put them together under a 'miscellaneous' heading is in no way intended to denigrate them; some are invaluable.

C. M. White: *Sources of Information in the Social Sciences: a Guide to the Literature.* Bedminster Press, N.J., 1964.

Forty-six pages on sociology specifically, with suggestions for basic books in various fields of sociology, plus lists of bibliographies, statistics, journals etc. Mainly American in perspective but worth using.

W. Belson and C. R. Bell: *A Bibliography of Papers bearing on the Adequacy of Techniques used in Survey Research.* The Market Research Society, London, 1960.

Forty pages of papers listed alphabetically by author; list of sixty-six journals referred to; four pages of references grouped by subject; three pages of reference books.

A. F. Wells: *The Local Social Survey in Great Britain*. Allen & Unwin, London, 1935.

A little-known but most interesting short history of the growth of 'the social survey movement'. Eighty-eight pages and a very useful bibliography of early surveys.

M. Abrams: *Social Surveys and Social Action*. Heinemann, London, 1951.

Useful short book giving historical aspects of social research in Britain, with chapters on pioneering work in poverty, market research, public opinion etc.

D. Caradog Jones: *Social Surveys*. Hutchinson, London, 1949.

A general survey of most survey researches in Britain up to the end of the 1939–45 war. Particularly good for its precis of studies of poverty.

R. Silvey: *The Measurement of Audiences*. B.B.C. Lunch-time Lectures—4th series, no. 4, B.B.C., London, 1966.

The head of B.B.C. audience research explains some of the problems of studying broadcasting audiences and explains the differences between the B.B.C. approach and the T.A.M. system.

Market Research Society Ltd.: *Social Class Definition in Market Research*. The Market Research Society, London, 1963.

Critical assessment of self-rating definitions, definitions based on occupation and/or subjective criteria, national food survey, census of population, readership-based and multi-dimensional definitions. Technical but worth trying for a good exercise in practical problems.

J. Gould and W. L. Kolb: *A Dictionary of the Social Sciences*. Tavistock, London, 1964, p. 761.

Dictionaries are as useful as you make them. If you do find one useful this one would be my choice.

Nels Anderson: *Our Industrial Urban Civilization*. Asia Publishing House, London and New York, 1964.

The main book is not relevant but eleven pages of 'Notes on Community Research' at the end are a model of clarity on the processes of research work.

E. Greenwood: *Experimental Sociology*. King's Crown Press, N.Y., 1945.

A very good general survey of the early attempts at developing experimental methods in sociological research. Describes most of the pioneer work, including F. S. Chapin.

Index